Male Supremacy
in the Catholic Church

An Insider's View

Roy Bourgeois
Catholic Priest for Forty Years

Editing, design, and production: Thomas P. Fenton and Mary J. Heffron, with assistance from John Drew

Cover image: dpa picture alliance/Alamy stock photo. A cardinal puts on his mitre during the religious mass "Pro Eligendo Romano Pontifice" in Saint Peter's Basilica in the Vatican, Vatican City, 12 March 2013.

Notes on terminology:

Maryknoll - There are currently four expressions of Maryknoll, namely, Maryknoll Society (priests and Brothers); Maryknoll Congregation (Sisters); Maryknoll Lay Missioners; and Maryknoll Affiliates. Unless specified otherwise below, references to "Maryknoll" mean the Maryknoll Society.

Catholic Church - Unless specified otherwise below, references to the "Catholic Church" mean the Roman Catholic Church.

Contents

Part One. Confronting Ignorance: My Own and That of My Country

Part Two. An Injustice Closer to Home

Foreword

"There is neither male nor female. In Christ you are one."
— Galatians 3:28

"Men are the authentic teachers of faith and morals."
— Cardinal William Levada, former head of the
Vatican's Congregation for the Doctrine of the Faith

The Roman Catholic Church and its all-male priesthood is a patriarchy—ruled and dominated by men. These men claim that they are the consecrated ones, chosen by God to govern the Church. They believe that only men can interpret the Bible and know the will of God.

Webster's New World College Dictionary defines hypocrisy as "pretending to be what one is not" and "a pretense of virtue and piety."

This book is about the hypocrisy of the patriarchy that rules and dominates the Catholic Church. As a Catholic priest, I was a member of this all-boys club for forty years.

Acknowledgments

This memoir is in memory of my dear parents, who by their love for each other brought me into the world and taught me the meaning of unconditional love.

It is also dedicated to the people of Vietnam and Latin America and the women in the Catholic Church who became my teachers and taught me that *solidarity* means making the struggle of others *your* struggle. This memoir is written in the hope that the men in the all-male priesthood, who dominate the church, will one day soon break their silence and call for the ordination of women.

Introduction

As a Roman Catholic priest, I found meaning, joy, and support in my ministry. One day, however, I did the unspeakable: I called for the ordination of women. This angered not only many of my fellow priests but also then Pope Benedict XVI. I received a letter from the Vatican stating that I was "causing grave scandal" in the church and that I must recant my public support for the ordination of women. For me, this was not possible. Believing that women and men are created of equal worth and dignity and that both are called by an all-loving God to serve as priests, my conscience would not allow me to recant. Therefore, in 2012, after serving as a Catholic priest for forty years, I was expelled from the priesthood and my religious community of longtime friends.

> *"Education is a progressive discovery of our own ignorance."*
> – Will Durant, American historian

I grew up in a small town in Louisiana. My parents, like the majority in the town, were hard-working, traditional Catholics. I attended a segregated public school and worshipped in a Catholic Church that was segregated.

After leaving college with a degree in geology, I became a naval officer and thought of making the military a career. In my fourth year of military service, the leaders of my country and church told us we had to go to Vietnam "to stop the spread of godless communism." I did not question them. I volunteered for duty in Vietnam, believing that the cause was noble and I would be doing God's work.

Vietnam became a turning point in my life. In the midst of all the violence and suffering, I started praying the rosary each day and, when possible, attended Mass.

One day I met a Catholic missionary priest from Canada who was caring for about 150 children at a nearby orphanage. Their parents had been killed by our bombs, bullets, and napalm.

In all the insanity and inhumanity of war, this humble priest stood out as a peacemaker, a healer. Spending time at the orphanage and getting to know the children, this priest, and the hard-working staff opened my eyes to the concept of solidarity.

When my year of service in Vietnam came to an end, I was discharged from the military. Grateful to be alive, I returned to my loving parents, three siblings, and numerous nieces and nephews in Louisiana.

After a wonderful visit with family and friends, I entered a seminary and began my studies for the priesthood. I was accepted into the Maryknoll Society, a missionary order headquartered in Ossining, New York. Maryknoll missionaries serve the poor in Asia, Africa, and Latin America.

After six years of study, I was ordained a Catholic priest in 1972. I finally found the meaning and hope I was seeking in life.

After becoming a priest, I went to Vietnam with a "Letter of Apology," which I gave to hundreds of Vietnamese. The letter said:

> *Many years ago, in the United States, our leaders told us we had to go to war in Vietnam. I was a young man and did not question them. I, and so many like me, went to your country knowing so little about you, your history, and your culture.*
>
> *I have returned to your country to apologize for all the suffering and death we caused.*

Over the years, I have asked for God's forgiveness for what we did. I now ask for yours.

I was humbled by the kindness and many expressions of forgiveness that I received from the people, including government and military leaders. I was especially inspired by a Buddhist monk, who, after reading my letter of apology, said, "Our greatest enemy in life is ignorance. Our weapon must be wisdom."

This short memoir is about discovering and confronting ignorance—my own, that of my country, and that of my church.

Where there is injustice, silence is complicity. For many years, in my ignorance, I was silent.

It took the madness and horror of Vietnam to awaken me and send me on my journey of resistance against injustice. I must confess that it was much easier for me to break my silence about the injustice of my country's foreign policy. As a "good and obedient" Catholic, I found it more difficult to speak out against the injustice in my church.

The first part of my memoir is about the people of Vietnam and Latin America who became my teachers and educated me about how my country was causing untold suffering and death in their countries.

They taught me the meaning of that all-important word, *solidarity*: making the struggle of others your struggle. Living out this call to solidarity led to my being expelled from Bolivia and spending four years in US federal prisons—and, later, to my expulsion from the priesthood.

The second part of my memoir is about the devout, intelligent, and courageous women in the Roman Catholic Church who are called by God to be priests but are rejected by an all-male clergy who rule and dominate the church.

I underestimated the depth of sexism and misogyny among my fellow priests. Throughout my ministry, they had supported me when I spoke out against racism, oppression, exploitation, militarism, bullying, and other injustices. They even supported me when I went to prison for nonviolent protests against US foreign policy in Latin America.

By addressing the injustice of sexism and gender inequality in our church, however, I had poked the beehive of patriarchy.

Catholic priests say that the call to priesthood comes from God. I began to ask my fellow priests and myself: "Who are we, as men, to say that our call from God is authentic, but God's call to women is not?"

When I called for the ordination of women and participated in a woman's ordination, the majority of my fellow priests (and the Vatican) were outraged. I had done the unspeakable. For some, I had joined the enemy. A few longtime priest friends confided in private that they supported me, but would not publicly call for women's ordination.

Polls show that the majority of Catholics in the United States support having women priests in their churches. They believe, as I do, that the problem is not with God, but with an all-male clerical culture that views women as lesser beings than men. It saddens me that the majority of Catholic priests I know and have worked with for forty years see women as a threat to their power.

Being expelled from the priesthood for trying to reform the Catholic Church was very painful. I had never before experienced such rejection. But I have no regrets about what I did. This experience gave me a glimpse of what millions of people go through every day on a much deeper level because of their race, gender, or sexual orientation.

The Catholic Church professes that we are all made

in the image of God. In our ignorance and prejudice toward others, however, we often make God in our image.
And that God, for many Catholics, is white, male, and
heterosexual. My memoir also addresses the cruelty, ignorance, and heresy of the Catholic Church's teaching
on homosexuality.

❑

Part One

Confronting Ignorance:
My Own and That of My Country

Chapter 1

Segregated: The Starting Point

WHEN WE COME INTO THIS WORLD, we have no say in where we are born, nor do we choose our race or gender.

I happened to be born a white male in a small Cajun town along the Mississippi River in Louisiana. The majority of the people in town were hard working, traditional Catholics. While the church leaders, all white men, told us that an all-loving God created everyone in our town and world equal, we did not live that out in our daily lives.

For twelve years, I attended a segregated public school and worshipped in a Catholic Church that reserved the last five pews for Black Catholics. We justified our prejudice by saying this was "our tradition" and that we were "separate but equal." During all those years, I cannot remember one white person—not a priest, teacher, parent, or student (myself included)—who dared to say, "There is a real problem here, and it's called racism."

In high school, football was my passion. My teammates and I were very influenced by our coach, a retired Navy commander, who taught us that character was made on the five-yard line in a tie game with two minutes to go.

Looking back, winning football games was everything. During football season, our coach told us to distance ourselves from our girlfriends so we could concentrate more on meeting our opponents on Friday night. I must say that, although we were small-town, docile, and naive young men, this was one command from our coach that we did not obey.

At the senior year football banquet, accompanied by my loving and hard-working parents, I was awarded the "Most Gritty" trophy. In my little Cajun world, it was like getting the Heisman Trophy.

When I graduated from high school in 1956, most of my friends and teammates went to Louisiana State University (LSU) in Baton Rouge, only forty miles away, so they could return home for the Friday night football games. I decided to attend the University of Louisiana in Lafayette, three hours away, knowing that, if I returned to be with my girlfriend on weekends and attend the Friday night football games, I would never finish college.

At the University of Louisiana, home of the Ragin' Cajuns, I worked hard and earned a degree in geology. I paid for my tuition by working during the summer as a roughneck on oil rigs in the Gulf of Mexico.

In my last year at the university, I fell in love with a coed from New Orleans who was the first activist I had ever met. She led a group of students at the university who were working to integrate the student center. I had never met anyone who was so courageous and outspoken about the injustice of racism.

Although we talked about marriage and a future together, it was not to be. When we graduated, she returned to New Orleans to pursue her career, and I left for Navy Officer Candidate School in Newport, Rhode Island. The Navy was my ticket out of Louisiana, an opportunity to explore the world before returning as a geologist and getting rich in the oil fields.

After graduating from Navy Officer Candidate School, I spent two years aboard ship traveling throughout the Caribbean Sea before being assigned to a NATO base in Athens, Greece. While in Greece, I decided to volunteer for shore duty in Vietnam. Vietnam would become a turning point in my life.

❑

Chapter 2

Vietnam: The Turning Point

I WAS VERY HAPPY WITH MY ASSIGNMENT as a naval officer to the NATO Communication Station in Athens, Greece. I traveled on my days off, enjoying the Greek hospitality, food, and ouzo (a Greek liqueur).

Greece was a two-year assignment. I had another year to go before completing my fourth year in the military and being discharged. I considered forsaking geology and making the military my career.

Then came the message from the Pentagon asking for volunteers for shore duty in Vietnam. After thinking about it for a couple of days, I decided to sign up. Close friends advised me against going, but I believed it was the right thing for me to do.

The leaders of our country and a number of Catholic bishops were saying that we had to go to war "to stop the spread of godless communism." I remember thinking that if we didn't stop the communist enemy in Vietnam, we would have to fight them on the shores of California.

I was also inspired by the words of President John F. Kennedy: "And so, my fellow Americans: ask not what your country can do for you—ask what you can do for your country." I must admit, I also viewed going to Vietnam as an opportunity to see another part of the world. Little did I know the impact this choice would have on my life.

En route to Vietnam from Greece, I stopped in Louisiana for a visit with my family. While supporting me in my decision, they were more concerned than I had anticipated. Touched, but undaunted, I proceeded toward my destiny.

The next stop was San Diego, California, for a week of weapons training, followed by a week of survival training in Hawaii. It was during this challenging training that I began to think about the seriousness of my decision to volunteer for duty in Vietnam. I don't know if it would have changed my decision, but I wish I had met that Buddhist monk before I went to his country. His words have frequently come to mind as I have journeyed through life. How true they are: "Our greatest enemy in life is ignorance." In our ignorance, we went to Vietnam believing that we were liberators. We later learned that the Vietnamese people saw us as invaders.

Full of new, gung-ho recruits, our plane arrived in Saigon during the big troop buildup in the summer of 1965. General William Westmoreland met us at the airport and promised that if we gave it our best shot, we would be home for Christmas. As it turned out, most of those who did make it home by Christmas arrived in body bags.

I was assigned to a small base upcountry in Qui Nhon. Our mission was to stop the flow of arms from the North. Not long after I arrived in Qui Nhon, my good friend from survival training, Ray Ellis, was killed while on patrol in the Mekong Delta.

After six months in Qui Nhon, I was transferred to the Navy Command Headquarters in Saigon. I welcomed the transfer, thinking I'd be safer in Saigon. I had

Receiving the Purple Heart from Admiral N.G. Ward

not yet learned that there was no safe place in Vietnam.

Not long after I arrived in Saigon, the Viet Cong attacked our officers' quarters, killing several officers and wounding more than a hundred. I was lucky. I was one of the wounded.

Throughout Vietnam were orphanages for children whose parents were killed in the war by our bombs, bullets, and napalm. One day, I met a Catholic missionary priest from Quebec, Canada, who was to have a big impact on my life. Father Lucien Olivier and a staff of two nuns who were also registered nurses, along with a few teachers and others, were caring for about 150 children at an orphanage on the outskirts of Saigon. I had never met a priest like Father Olivier. He was humble and filled with compassion, and he stood out in the midst of all the suffering and death in Vietnam.

The children at the orphanage were Buddhists, but he had no interest in converting them to Catholicism. Father Olivier and his hard-working coworkers at the orphanage were all about loving and trying to heal the suffering of vulnerable children who were innocent victims of ignorance and war.

Among the orphans were toddlers who longed to be held, and older children, some of them malnourished and dressed in rags. In short, life at this orphanage—as at most orphanages throughout the country—was a struggle for survival.

I started recruiting some of my buddies from our base to come to the orphanage with me. Some of them had children of their own back home and were deeply touched by the orphans. It didn't take long before we

Visiting children at Fr. Olivier's orphanage

started bringing jeeploads of supplies for the children and making badly needed repairs on the buildings that housed them.

One day, my commanding officer called me in and told me that I was spending too much time at the orphanage. He reminded me that we were in Vietnam to fight a war, not take care of children. Needless to say, that was one command I could not obey.

I had volunteered for duty in Vietnam thinking that I would make the military a career. As my year of military service was coming to an end, I realized that this was no longer an option.

After much prayer and reflection, I spoke to an Army chaplain about becoming a Catholic priest and doing missionary work like Father Olivier. The chaplain recommended that I contact the Maryknoll Missionary Order, headquartered in Ossining, New York. Maryknoll's priests, Brothers, and Sisters serve the poor in Asia, Africa, and Latin America.

My long and challenging year in Vietnam came to an end, and I was heading back home to Louisiana. When the plane departed Saigon, many of us wept. They were tears of joy. We were alive, and we were going home to be with our loved ones. It was a new beginning filled with hope.

❑

Chapter 3

Preparing for the Priesthood
– Women Need Not Apply

A FTER A WONDERFUL VISIT with family and friends, I began my studies for the priesthood. The next six years exceeded my expectations as I found the meaning, joy, peace, and hope I was seeking in life.

I spent my first year at Maryknoll's college in Glen Ellyn, Illinois, where I studied philosophy. This was followed by a year of "spiritual formation" at the Novitiate in Hingham, Massachusetts. Then came four years of theological studies, prayer, and reflection at Maryknoll's major seminary in Ossining, New York.

After my first year at the major seminary in New York, during the summer of 1968, I was assigned to do volunteer work with the inner-city poor in various cities in the United States.

It was a long shot, but I asked the rector of the seminary if I could spend the summer working at Father Olivier's orphanage in Vietnam instead. To my surprise, he granted me permission, but told me I would have to pay for my own airfare, which was quite expensive.

Determined to see the children and Father Olivier

again, I was able to get a newspaper in Vermont, the *Burlington Free Press*, to pay for my airfare in exchange for my agreement to write an article for the paper about the plight of the orphans in Vietnam.

Months before I left for Vietnam, the Tet offensive took place. The North Vietnamese army and their Viet Cong allies launched attacks in more than forty South Vietnamese cities, including Saigon. The offensive was repelled, but Tet shook public support in the United States for the war.

When I arrived in Saigon, Father Olivier informed me that the children at the orphanage had had to be evacuated during the fighting and were sent to orphanages elsewhere in the country. Thankfully, all of the children had gotten out safely.

I ended up spending most of my summer in Vietnam driving a truck for Catholic Relief Services, delivering badly needed supplies to refugee camps on the outskirts of Saigon.

I returned to the seminary feeling more committed than ever to becoming a priest and working for peace.

I received an invitation from the *Burlington Free Press* to go to Vermont and give a talk about Vietnam to the newspaper's staff and general public. I joined many in our country who were then calling for our troops to stop the killing and come home.

I continued my seminary studies, and I was grateful for the peace and meaning I had in my life. At the same time, I often found it difficult to be studying theology in a classroom and praying in a chapel when millions of people around the country were in the streets, protesting the war.

During my fifth year in the seminary, I decided to join a group of my classmates and two priests on our faculty who were going to Washington, DC, to protest against the war. It was my first protest ever and, after

Maryknoll ordination class of 1972 with Terence Cardinal Cooke

much discernment, I decided to join about one hundred protesters who participated in a "die in" in front of the White House. We were all arrested and spent the night in jail.

Somehow, I saw spending that night in a small cell as a sacred moment in my life. I was finally learning that when there is an injustice, silence is consent. I was finally discovering that I had a voice, and it was time for me to start using it for peace.

When we returned to the seminary from Washington, our group decided to run a paid advertisement in the local Westchester County newspaper, calling for the United States to end the war and bring the troops home. Ninety percent of the seminarians and priests on the faculty signed the ad, which gave us hope.

At the end of my sixth year of studies, on May 27, 1972, ten of us were ordained Catholic priests at the Maryknoll seminary by Terence Cardinal Cooke. Our families and friends were present, and it was a wonderful, joyful occasion.

Similar to returning from Vietnam, ordination was a new beginning, a leap into the unknown. Months before our ordination, we had received our assignments. I was assigned to serve the poor of Bolivia.

Reflecting on my six years in the seminary, I always felt grateful to be with such kind, compassionate, and good-hearted classmates and faculty. There was always a feeling of sadness when one of my classmates made a decision to leave.

Many did leave. When I entered the seminary, there were more than three hundred men preparing for the priesthood in the Maryknoll order. Today, there are eighteen.

As I look back now on my studies in the seminary and my decades as a priest, I can understand why the Catholic priesthood is going out of existence.

At the root of the problem is the Catholic Church's treatment of women as inferior to men. So much of what we were taught in the seminary contributed to our sexism and misogyny as priests. I regret to say that our training encouraged us to view women as a threat to our vocation. Like Eve in the Bible, women were "the temptress." I will never forget the priest who often reminded us about the importance of "custody of the eyes" when it came to women.

In the seminary, we often read Bible passages that depicted women as inferior to men, as in 1 Timothy 2:12–13, which states: "I permit no woman to teach or to have authority over men. She is to keep silent."

Then there were the writings of the Church Fathers, which were mandatory reading. Saint Augustine, for example, viewed women as intellectually inferior and as a moral threat to men. And there was Saint Thomas Aquinas, who wrote in *Summa Theologica*: "Since any supremacy of rank cannot be expressed in the female sex, which has the status of an inferior, that sex cannot be ordained."

The official teaching of the Roman Catholic Church states that only baptized males can be ordained as priests. The church's justification for the all-male priesthood is that Jesus chose twelve *men* as his apostles.

The teaching does not mention that there is absolutely no evidence in the Bible that Jesus ordained anyone, male or female. There is reference to the twelve apostles, who are married lay followers of Jesus. They are never referred to as priests.

We do read in Scripture that Jesus' faithful followers were called elders, workers of the Gospel, emissaries, evangelists, teachers, prophets, miracle workers, and shepherds. Every one of these ministries was filled by both men and women.

Our professors in the seminary did not mention the women apostles of the early church. For example, in Romans 16:7, Paul refers to a woman by the name of Junia, who was imprisoned for spreading the faith, as a "highly distinguished apostle." And let us not forget Mary Magdalene, the first person Jesus appeared to after his resurrection. She was commissioned to bring the good news to the male apostles—who were hiding behind locked doors out of fear. Mary Magdalene became known as "the apostle to the apostles."

In our seminary training, we often heard that only men can be priests because Jesus was a man; therefore, only a man can represent Him at the Mass. This is ignorance at its worst! Jesus was also a Jew. Shouldn't that also be a requirement for priesthood?

In the seminary, we never discussed the possibility of women priests.

The message was clear: As men, we were being called by God to do something that women could not do. We were going to be Catholic priests, the consecrated ones, the "authentic teachers of faith and morals."

By the time we were ordained, we had gotten a good taste of what it felt like to be put on a pedestal. Little did we know that our ordination was only the beginning of what would become an addiction—an addiction to power.

It was admirable that we loved God and wanted to spend the rest of our lives serving the poor of the world. But something happened to us. We developed an addiction to power. Over time, we began to view women as a threat to that power and privilege.

❏

Chapter 4

Serving in a Bolivian Slum

AFTER MY ORDINATION IN NEW YORK, my family and I returned to Louisiana for my first Mass.

During the Mass and at the reception afterwards, it was a joy to see relatives, friends, and high school classmates I had not seen for years, including my high school girlfriend. Years ago we had planned a future together, but like so many of our plans and dreams in life, it was not to be.

After a great visit with my family and a few fishing trips with my brother, I departed for my mission assignment to Bolivia. There I joined more than one hundred Maryknoll priests and nuns serving the poor. Many had been in Bolivia for years, and I was profoundly inspired by their deep faith, simple lifestyles, and commitment to the poor.

First stop in Bolivia was the Maryknoll language school in Cochabamba, where I studied Spanish for four months. I must confess that I was one of the worst students to ever attend the school. When I spoke Spanish, Bolivians actually thought I was speaking some indigenous language.

Falling ill with typhoid fever during my third month

With Aymara women in their cooperative near La Paz

of studies was an even greater challenge. At the hospital, where I spent a week, I began to wonder whether I was cut out to live and work with the poor of Bolivia.

Thanks to the dedicated teachers at the school and the great doctors at the hospital, I was able to graduate from language school.

Maryknoll assigned me to a slum on the outskirts of La Paz. This community became my home for the next five years, and it was here that the poor and oppressed became my teachers and friends, showing me the meaning of solidarity.

For the majority of Bolivians, life was a struggle for survival. As in Vietnam, I was humbled by the people who had so little and suffered so much, yet held on to their hope for a better life.

Celebrating Mass in Bolivia

As always, my family back in Louisiana was very supportive of my work and raised a lot of money for various health and educational projects in the slum.

As a US citizen in Bolivia, I was angry to see my country supporting a brutal military dictator, General Hugo Banzer, who came to power through a violent coup. And I was sad to see my own country exploiting Bolivia's cheap labor and the country's vast natural resources, as the conquistadors had done centuries ago.

People who are oppressed and exploited, who watch their children die before their time, do what we would do if we lived under such conditions. They start organizing, walking in solidarity with each other, and speaking out for life and justice. When they do, however, those with the power, wealth, and guns retaliate swiftly and harshly. Many are killed or imprisoned.

During my fourth year in Bolivia, it became clear that I could not be a traditional Catholic priest who just said Mass, baptized babies, and officiated at marriages and funerals. After much discernment and prayer, I made a decision to break my silence and join the poor in their resistance against the violence and brutality of the military dictatorship.

As a result, during my fifth year in Bolivia, I was arrested and forced to leave the country.

❑

Chapter 5

Off to the Killing Fields of El Salvador

RETURNING TO THE UNITED STATES after living in a Bolivian slum for five years was a big adjustment. While it was wonderful to see my family and friends again, I missed the people of Bolivia, who had become such an important part of my life and ministry.

After spending time with my Maryknoll community in Ossining, New York, I went to the Bolivian Embassy in New York City to inquire about getting a visa. After they saw "Prohibido Entrar" stamped in my passport, I was informed that this was not possible.

That night I walked aimlessly through the streets of New York City, feeling like a stranger in my own country. Leaning against a skyscraper in the middle of a city with millions of people, feeling so alone, I wept.

As a priest, I found such meaning and strength in the Psalms, especially during challenging times. Psalm 30 says, "Weeping may spend the night, but joy comes in the morning."

My joy did return, but like so many struggles we experience in life, it took longer than waiting for morning.

I went to Washington, DC, to attend a seminar organized by the Network Lobby for Catholic Social Justice on how to lobby members of Congress on US foreign policy issues. At this seminar I met many kindred spirits who helped me realize that there was much work to be done in my own country.

After a sabbatical that included my enrollment in a number of courses on Latin America, I was assigned to Maryknoll's Development Department house in Chicago in 1979. It was here, in my ministry with fellow Maryknoll priests, that the meaning and hope I once had in life returned. My ministry involved giving talks at colleges and high schools during the week, and on weekends I would visit Catholic churches to say Mass, give sermons, hear confessions, and raise money for our mission work in Latin America, Asia, and Africa. In my work, I felt connected to the poor of Bolivia and frequently met people who gave me hope in the struggle for peace and justice.

Then the unexpected happened, making the front pages of newspapers across the country. On March 24, 1980, Archbishop Oscar Romero was assassinated in El Salvador for championing the rights of the poor. Months later, four American churchwomen were raped and killed by the Salvadoran military: Ursuline nun Dorothy Kazel, lay missionary Jean Donovan, and two Maryknoll nuns who were my friends, Maura Clarke and Ita Ford. What happened to these four women and Archbishop Romero brought the war in El Salvador closer to home for many of us.

With the support of my fellow priests, I went on a human rights delegation to El Salvador to learn more about the situation in this small country of five million people.

I had never seen anything quite like El Salvador. The country was controlled and dominated by a small, wealthy elite: the so-called fourteen families, who owned 60 percent of the most fertile land. While these families lived in mansions and were waited on by their servants, the poor and oppressed of the country made a dollar a day picking coffee beans for export to the United States. They and their children were malnourished and lacked basic medical care. For the majority of the people in El Salvador, life was a struggle for survival.

As in Bolivia, the United States was on the side of the military and wealthy elite who protected America's economic interests. In a real sense, we were the new conquistadors. US and Salvadoran leaders blamed the war on communism. The people we met, however, said that the problem was not communism, but rather the human condition of suffering. They said that the vast majority of Salvadorans were hungry and doing what US citizens would do if their children lived in such poverty. Like the Salvadoran people, we too would resist and speak out for food and a living wage for our labor.

Our delegation learned that the Salvadoran military targeted and killed Archbishop Romero and the four churchwomen because they dared to walk in solidarity with the poor and oppressed of the country.

Like everyone else on our delegation, I returned to Chicago feeling I had a responsibility to speak out about the untold suffering and death the United States was causing in El Salvador.

Most people in our country did not know that the United States was funneling a million dollars a day—all from our tax money—to the Salvadoran military, which was at war with its people. Once again, I saw that our greatest enemy in life is ignorance. The good news, however, is that most people have good hearts filled with compassion. And when they learn about the needless suffering and death of others, they respond.

The following year I was assigned to Maryknoll's Development center in New Orleans and continued fundraising for the order. Being in New Orleans was a gift, as I was able to see my family more often.

Vigil at entrance of Fort Benning, Georgia

While I was going about my work in the Big Easy, once again something happened that disturbed our "business as usual" routine. The *New York Times* reported that 525 Salvadoran soldiers had arrived at Fort Benning, Georgia, for combat training.

Knowing the consequences of this training to the poor of El Salvador, I contacted Maryknoll headquarters in New York and got their permission to go to Fort Benning with others and protest this combat training. In Columbus, Georgia, home of Fort Benning, I was joined by Larry Rosebaugh, a Catholic priest with the Missionary Oblates of Mary Immaculate, and Linda Ventimiglia. Larry had worked for years with the poor of Brazil, and Linda, a former army reserve officer from Alabama, had worked at a Catholic Worker house in Texas.

We rented a small house, called it Casa Romero, and began reflecting on what we should do about the Salvadoran soldiers at Fort Benning. Within days, we were joined by others, including a few Vietnam veterans.

Larry and I visited a number of priests at local Catholic churches, requesting permission to give presentations about Archbishop Romero and the four churchwomen to their congregations. Most priests said that their congregations included active duty and retired military personnel, and our message would be "too controversial." Two priests, however, did allow us to give presentations in their churches, which gave us hope.

One day, as we went about our work, we received a tape recording in the mail, sent to us by friends at the Catholic Worker house in Chicago. It was Archbishop Oscar Romero's last sermon, given in the cathedral of San Salvador on March 23, 1980. His words so infuriated the military that he was killed the next day while saying Mass.

That night at Casa Romero, we all came together and listened to the words of this courageous man:

> *I would like to make a special appeal to the military. Brothers, each one of you is one of us. We are the same people. The peasants you kill are your own brothers and sisters. When you hear the voice of a man commanding you to kill, remember instead the voice of God: THOU SHALL NOT KILL!*

No soldier is obliged to obey an order contrary to the law of God.

In the name of God, in the name of our tormented people whose cries rise up to heaven, I beseech you, I beg you, I command you, stop the repression!

After listening to Archbishop Romero's last sermon, we knew what we had to do. We would go to Fort Benning and play the words of this holy man for those Salvadoran soldiers being trained to kill.

The next day Linda, Larry, and I bought a powerful tape player and then went to an army surplus store where we bought uniforms. We spent a few days practicing climbing trees in a nearby pine forest and testing our high-powered cassette player with four speakers. Finally, we were ready: It was "All systems go!"

A couple of days later, at dusk, the three of us, dressed as high-ranking army officers, entered Fort Benning with all our equipment packed in a Land Rover (with a Fort Benning sticker). The driver, a Vietnam vet, let us off near the barracks housing the 525 Salvadoran soldiers.

In the darkness, Linda, Larry, and I scaled a tall pine tree, secured the tape player, and waited. When the last lights went out in the barracks, we pressed down on the button and said, "Brother Oscar Romero, this is for you." His voice boomed into the barracks, telling the soldiers to stop their killing.

The lights came on, sirens wailed, and soldiers with M-16 rifles swarmed the grounds with dogs. As Romero's words continued to boom throughout the area, it didn't take long for them to locate us. Soldiers congregated under our tree with their weapons of war and dogs, threatening to shoot us if we did not come down. It was time to come down. But we left the tape player in the tree—repeating the words of Romero:

*In the name of God, in the name of our tormented
people whose cries rise up to heaven, I beseech you, I beg
you, I command you, stop the repression!*

When we came down, we were roughed up, handcuffed, and taken to military police headquarters, where
we were questioned by the FBI and Fort Benning
officials. Linda, Larry, and I carried no identification on
us. When questioned, Linda gave her name as Jean Donovan, one of the four US churchwomen raped and murdered by the Salvadoran military. Larry gave his name as
Rutilio Grande, a Jesuit priest slain by the military. And I
gave my name as Oscar Romero.

In the midst of their many questions, we had nothing
to hide. We simply said that what we did was a humble
act of solidarity with the people of El Salvador, who are
being killed by their military, armed and trained by our
country.

The three of us were charged with criminal trespass
and impersonating military officers and taken to the
Muscogee County Jail in Columbus, Georgia, then to
trial.

US District Court Judge J. Robert Elliott, nicknamed
"Maximum Bob," officiated at our trial. He was a
well-known segregationist who had barred Dr. Martin
Luther King Jr. from leading a civil rights march in
Georgia. Judge Elliott had also overturned the murder
conviction of William Calley, the army lieutenant
court-martialed for his role in the My Lai massacre during the Vietnam War.

The packed courtroom was filled with family and
friends. It was good to have my parents, two sisters, and
brother there, but it hurt to see them worried about the
consequences of what we did. While it is important for
us to live our own lives and be true to our own experiences in life and where that might lead us, sometimes it's

difficult for others to understand our actions.

While I know my family and some friends were struggling to comprehend what we did at Fort Benning, I was grateful and humbled by their unconditional love and support. It also meant a lot to me to see many long-time priest friends in the courtroom from my Maryknoll community who had supported our action.

During the trial, it was tough going with Judge Elliott, who refused to hear anything from us about the killing fields of El Salvador, Archbishop Romero, the four churchwomen, or US military aid to El Salvador. We were found guilty of criminal trespass and impersonating army officers. Linda and Larry were sentenced to fifteen months in prison, and I got eighteen months. Linda served her time at a federal prison in Lexington, Kentucky; Larry went to a prison in La Tuna, Texas; I was sent to a prison in Terre Haute, Indiana.

❏

Chapter 6

Prison

WHEN I ARRIVED AT THE FEDERAL PRISON in Terre Haute, I was informed that all inmates were required to work and would receive twelve cents an hour for their labor.

A couple of days later, I was assigned to clean the offices of prison offcials, which presented a problem. For me, the problem was not being made to work or being paid twelve cents an hour. Rather, it was that I was imprisoned for a nonviolent protest, while Salvadoran soldiers who had killed poor people and religious leaders walked free.

I decided to go on strike. I told prison offcials that I would gladly work when those who killed Archbishop Oscar Romero and raped and killed the four church-women started serving their time. There was no discussion. I was immediately handcuffed and taken to solitary confinement, also known as "the hole," where I spent the next month alone in a six-by-nine-foot cell.

Being a great lover of solitude, I thought I had received an unexpected vacation. Like most people I know, I have a need for alone time after a busy day. One of my favorite psalms is Psalm 46, which says: "Be still and know that I am God." During my frst week in the hole, I felt a deep inner peace in this cell with no windows and where food arrived through a small slot between steel bars.

Then something changed. My inner peace was shattered, and I started feeling very alone. I began to question the effectiveness of our protest at Fort Benning and wondered if anything had changed as a result of what Linda, Larry, and I had done. Just days after our trial, the Associated Press reported that Salvadoran soldiers had massacred more than a hundred civilians, including women and children.

During the next two weeks, God felt very distant. I could not pray and began to experience some dark nights of the soul.

Then came an insight that brought with it a ray of sunshine and some renewed hope. I started thinking about how our all-loving Creator doesn't ask us to be effective in what we do, but asks simply that we try to be faithful and love one another as God loves us.

Archbishop Romero addressed the issue of effectiveness versus faithfulness in one of his sermons. He said:

> *We accomplish in our lifetime only a tiny fraction of the magnificent enterprise that is God's work.*
>
> *We cannot do everything, and there is a sense of liberation in realizing that. This enables us to do something, and to do it very well.*
>
> *We may never see the end results, but that is the difference between the master builder and the worker. We are the workers, not the master builder; the ministers, not the messiah. We are the prophets of a future that is not our own.*

My fourth week in solitary confinement was like coming out of the desert. Happy thoughts, joy, and a deep inner peace had returned.

During the week, I received an unexpected visit from the prison's warden. He wanted to know how I was doing. I told him all was well and that I would like to serve the remainder of my sentence in solitary confinement. He said that was not possible, and that in two days, I would be transferred to the federal prison in Sandstone, Minnesota.

The long bus trip to Minnesota with fellow inmates, all of us in handcuffs, was pure bliss. After spending a month in the hole, it was wonderful to be outdoors again.

Serving out my sentence in Minnesota turned out much better than I had anticipated. My job in prison was to teach English to Hispanic inmates, including a few from El Salvador, who were doing heavy time for drug-related crimes.

Prison provides time for reading. As an activist, I was critical of Catholic contemplatives. But somehow this changed. As the months unfolded, I asked friends on "the outside" to send me the writings of the well-known Trappist monk Thomas Merton, along with those of Saint John of the Cross, Teresa of Avila, and the Desert Fathers of the fourth century. I devoured their writings, inspired by their humility, simple lifestyles, and quest to seek God on a deeper level.

At the same time, I still thought as an activist and realized that Judge Elliott could send me to prison, but he could not silence me. I wrote many letters to major newspapers around the country about our protest at Fort Benning and how the United States was complicit in the suffering and death in El Salvador. A number of my letters were published, which kept my hope alive.

Before going to prison, every year I would make a week's retreat at a monastery. This was a time to step back from my work and be still, reflect, pray, worship, and do some spiritual reading. In short, the annual retreat was about trying to purify the heart and get closer to our all-loving God and God's people.

I must admit that spending a year and a half in prison for our humble act of solidarity with the people of El Salvador turned out to be the best retreat I had ever made.

After much discernment, when I was released from prison, I told my family and Maryknoll community that I planned to enter a Trappist monastery and become a contemplative monk. Needless to say, they were rather surprised, but, as always, understanding and supportive.

Before entering the Trappist Monastery of the Holy Spirit in Conyers, Georgia, where I had made a number of retreats, I spent quality time with my family in Louisiana and with my fellow priests in New York. I also did some traveling and gave a few talks before "leaving the world" and entering the silence of the monastery.

❑

Chapter 7

From Prison to a Monastery: "The Way of Silence"

Anyone who delights in a multitude of words, even if they say admirable things, is empty within. Silence will illuminate you in God and deliver you from the phantoms of ignorance. Silence will unite you to God. More than all things love silence, for it brings you a fruit that the tongue cannot describe.

In the beginning we have to force ourselves to be silent. But then from our silence is born something that draws us into deeper silence. May God give you an experience of this "something" that is born of silence. If you practice this, inexpressible light will dawn upon you.

— Isaac of Nineveh

WHEN I ARRIVED AT THE TRAPPIST MONASTERY in Conyers, Georgia, I was very much at peace with my decision to live as a contemplative monk. I thought that my experiences in Vietnam, Bolivia, El Salvador, and prison were all leading me to this new vocation.

Fifty-five monks lived at the monastery. A number of them had been in the military or had jobs before entering. Many of the monks had spent decades in the monastery, and I felt honored to be in their presence.

Most people I know are very active. They fill their days with much activity and lots of work. Often, it's a challenge for parents and their families to get even a few minutes of quiet time during the day. The Trappists (formally known as the Order of Cistercians of the Strict Observance) are monks who feel their calling in life is to withdraw from the world and seek God as full-time contemplatives. Their daily life is spent in silence, private and communal prayer, and manual labor.

Life in the monastery was a rather big adjustment for me. We rose at 3:45 a.m. At 4:00 a.m., we gathered in the chapel to sing the psalms, followed by silent meditation. A light breakfast was served at 5:00 a.m. (in silence), followed by spiritual reading and Mass.

Then it was off to work. The Conyers monks sustain themselves by selling bread, bales of hay, ferns, Bonsai trees, and a large selection of spiritual books. At noon, the monks gather again for prayer and lunch. (Trappists are strictly vegetarian.) Lunch is followed by an hour of rest, and then it's back to work. At 5:30 p.m., we gather in the chapel for meditation, followed by dinner. After a final communal prayer, the monks observe the "Grand Silence," retiring at 8:30 p.m.

Being a night owl, it took a while to adjust to this new schedule. But after a few days, I started feeling at home in the monastery.

I arrived at the monastery as an activist priest, a protester. In a way, I had come to see the daily life of the monks as the ultimate protest. It was a rejection of worldly values of wealth and power. It was saying no to the false gods we worship in society today.

As a novice, I would meet twice a week with my novice master, a monk who had been in the monastery for thirty-five years. As my spiritual director, he asked me how I was adjusting to life in the monastery.

During the first two months, it was all positive. Going into my third month, doubts began to surface about spending the rest of my life as a contemplative monk. I began to miss my peace and justice work, as well as my family, friends, and Maryknoll community. I longed to know more about what was going on in the "outside world." Phone calls and visits were prohibited. Each day a few selected newspaper clippings were posted on a bulletin board, but after reading them, I wanted to know more.

In a way, I had more freedom in prison than I did in the monastery. In prison, we were allowed visitors, could make phone calls, and had access to newspapers.

While praying in the monastery chapel, I began asking myself questions: What would the people of Vietnam think if, upon leaving their country, I told them my prayers would be with them, but then did nothing to stop the war? Or the people in the slums of Bolivia if, as their priest, I said I was praying for them, but did not join them in speaking out against a brutal dictator my country supported? What would the suffering poor of El Salvador, a very Catholic country, say if I told them my thoughts and prayers were with them, but I did nothing to stop the killing?

During the next two months, it became clear that I was not cut out to be a full-time contemplative. Instead, I needed to balance my activism in the world with silence, solitude, and prayer.

I informed my novice master that my five months at the monastery had been very important to me, and that I had learned a lot, but it was now time to return to my ministry with Maryknoll.

And so, on a beautiful spring day in Georgia, I said goodbye to my monk friends and left the monastery. The azaleas were in full bloom, and birds were singing. I was returning to my work for peace and justice in the world, and I felt, once again, filled with hope and joy.

❑

Chapter 8

The Work of SOA Watch

I LEFT THE MONASTERY and went to Maryknoll headquarters in New York to spend a few days with the community, followed by some time in Louisiana with my family. No one was surprised that I had left the life of a monk.

Maryknoll assigned me to its Development Department house in Minneapolis, Minnesota, where I really felt at home. In the Twin Cities, I encountered many others speaking out against the injustice of US intervention in Central America. It was a joy to be with so many kindred spirits and find such meaning in my ministry.

On November 16, 1989, another massacre in El Salvador made the front pages of newspapers around the world. In the early morning, the Salvadoran military entered the Jesuit University of Central America in San Salvador and murdered six Jesuit priests, their housekeeper, and her teenage daughter. Like Archbishop Oscar Romero and the four churchwomen, these six priests were advocates for the poor and oppressed of the country.

The massacre generated tremendous anger in El Salvador and in the United States, especially because the US was giving millions of dollars to the Salvadoran military.

A Congressional task force was sent to El Salvador to investigate the massacre. They reported that those responsible for the massacre had been trained at the US Army School of the Americas (SOA) at Fort Benning, Georgia.

After much reflection and discussion with others, I decided it was important to return to Georgia and investigate the School of the Americas. Once again, my Maryknoll brothers came through with their support and solidarity.

I immediately went to work recruiting longtime activist friends around the country to join me. While I awaited their response, I drove to Columbus, Georgia, and rented an apartment outside of Fort Benning.

I was joined by friends: Kathy Kelly, a peace activist and schoolteacher from Chicago; Charlie Liteky, a recipient of the Congressional Medal of Honor in Vietnam from California; a Jesuit priest from Boston; two Dominican priests; two Salvadorans who had been forced to leave their country due to death threats; and one other

The fasters (from left to right): Fr. Brian Pierce, O.P.; Fr. Jack Seery, S.J.; René Hurtado; Miguel Cruz; Kathy Kelly; Fr. Bourgeois, M.M.; Fr. Jim Barnett, O.P.; Charlie Liteky; and Peter Eaves.

Male Supremacy in the Catholic Church

Vietnam veteran.

After a few days of reflection, the nine of us decided to camp out in front of the main entrance to Fort Benning for a thirty-five-day, water-only fast. We called it "A Fast for Peace in El Salvador." During our fast, Mary Swenson and Bill Barnett from Minneapolis were a great help to us, supplying us with plenty of water and doing media outreach.

As the days went by, our bodies grew weak, but our spirits remained strong.

The local newspaper, the Columbus *Ledger-Enquirer,* helped our cause by publishing a number of articles about our fast. Local supporters would visit us each day from 5:00 p.m. to 6:00 p.m., a time we designated for sharing reflections, prayer, and good music to uplift our spirits.

The newspaper also published a front-page article on Medal of Honor recipient Charlie Liteky, who had served as a Catholic chaplain in Vietnam. This article brought many soldiers at Fort Benning to the main gate, wanting to shake Charlie's hand. Some of the soldiers, fearful of being seen with us protesters, came late at night as we were asleep on the ground in our sleeping bags.

At the end of our thirty-five-day fast, food never tasted so good. We had all lost a lot of weight, but never lost our hope. Each day of the fast we reminded ourselves why we were standing vigilant at the gates of Fort Benning. It was about solidarity with others. We were also aware that our fast was voluntary, and we could end it at any time, while millions of our sisters and brothers in the world went without food every day. How could we not sacrifice food and stand in solidarity with our poor and oppressed brothers and sisters, suffering at the hands of American-trained oppressors?

When our fast ended, some of us decided to stay in

town to do some further research on the School of the Americas. We called our small group the SOA Watch.

We learned that the School of the Americas (SOA) had been founded in 1946 by the U.S. Army and initially located in Panama. Soldiers throughout Latin America attended this military school to learn combat skills, military intelligence, interrogation techniques (torture), psychological warfare, and counterinsurgency tactics.

People who are oppressed, exploited, and made to suffer will eventually resist and speak out. We learned in our research that the mission of the SOA was to train Latin American soldiers to suppress domestic dissent. In short, these soldiers were used to protect US exploitation of Latin America's cheap labor and the region's vast natural resources.

In the 1960s and 1970s, the SOA became known as La Escuela de Golpes, the School of Coups, because so many of its graduates had overthrown their democratically elected governments. General Hugo Banzer, the brutal dictator of Bolivia, who came into power through a violent coup, was not only an SOA grad but also a member of the school's Hall of Fame.

In an editorial calling for the school's closure, the Panamanian newspaper *La Prensa* dubbed it the "School of Assassins," while Panama's President Jorge Illueja called it "the biggest base for destabilization in Latin America."

In 1984, as a result of growing protests against the military school and under the terms of the Panama Canal Treaty, the SOA was expelled from Panama and quietly moved to Fort Benning, Georgia.

Our small group felt we had learned enough about this School of Assassins; it was time to act. In two weeks, it would be the first anniversary of the massacre of the mother, her teenage daughter, and the six Jesuit priests in El Salvador. Those who did the killing were trained at the SOA, just down the road from us.

So, here's what we did. On November 16, 1990, three of us, Charlie Liteky, his brother Patrick (who had trained at Fort Benning), and I drove to the headquarters of the School of Americas. At the entrance we placed a white cross with the names and photographs of the six Jesuit priests, the mother, and her daughter before we entered the lobby, which featured photographs of SOA graduates. To emphasize the bloodshed that graduates of this school were causing in El Salvador, the three of us sprinkled blood (our blood, drawn by a nurse and stored in small containers) on the photographs. We left a letter, signed by each of us, calling for the closing of the School of the Americas.

Within minutes, we were arrested, taken to jail, and charged with criminal trespass and destruction of government property.

Once again, "Maximum Bob" was the presiding judge. And, as before, he did not want to hear anything about American foreign policy, the SOA, or the killing fields of El Salvador. Nor was the jury interested in why we did what we did.

Our loved ones' presence in the courtroom helped us get through this difficult trial. It also meant a lot to me to have a number of my fellow priests from Maryknoll at the trial.

It took the jury only twenty-one minutes to return guilty verdicts. Charlie and Patrick were sentenced to six months in prison; I got sixteen months.

When people are sent to prison for a cause they believe in, they are very grateful when people on "the outside" join their cause and continue the work. Vicky Imerman was just such a person for us. Vicky was a college graduate from Iowa and had attended Officer Candidate School at Fort Benning. Now a civilian, Vicky had visited us during our fast and said that she would like to

A visit from my family at the federal prison in Tallahassee, FL, during a sixteen-month sentence for protesting the SOA. (l-r): My sister Janet, my father, Roy Sr., my sister Ann, my brother, Dan, and my mother, Grace.

continue our research on the SOA.

At the time, we did not realize the contribution Vicky would make to our movement, then in its infancy.

Vicky Imerman was a brilliant researcher. The SOA had refused to give her the names of the school's 55,000 graduates, but she found them on the website of the nonprofit National Security Archive. Using these names, she scanned human rights reports and news clippings that gave the names of Latin American military linked to atrocities. What she discovered was that hundreds of SOA graduates had participated in massacres, torture, rape, and military coups.

While I was serving my sixteen-month sentence at the federal prison in Tallahassee, Florida, Vicky would occasionally visit me and bring updates of her research. It was then that I realized how important it was for us to continue our work to close what really was a School of Assassins on US soil, all paid for by American taxpayers. For many years, this military school had been hiding behind a wall of secrecy. We knew so little about the history of the SOA. Once again, our enemy was ignorance. The goal of SOA Watch would be to tear down this wall and get the truth out to the general public, members of Congress, and the media.

For a grassroots movement to blossom and grow, it needs a lot of people doing a lot of different things. The goal of our movement was to close the US Army School of the Americas, which was causing untold suffering and death throughout Latin America. In that struggle, we learned that everyone can do something—and do it well.

The following is what many did to enable our SOA Watch movement to grow in numbers and spirit.

When Charlie, Patrick, and I were released from prison, we took Vicky Imerman's research on the SOA to colleges, churches, and peace groups around the country.

As the movement grew, and I continued to live in the apartment outside the entrance to Fort Benning, we realized it was important to open an SOA Watch office in Washington, DC. We could not have found a better person than Carol Richardson to open that office and gradually bring other staff members on board. Carol was a Methodist pastor and a skilled grassroots organizer who had worked with Witness for Peace before joining SOA Watch. Our SOA Watch website (soaw.org) along with our newsletter called *Presente!* brought many into the movement.

From the very beginning, we felt it was important to gather at the entrance of Fort Benning one weekend in November to call for the closing of the SOA and to keep alive the memories of those killed by SOA graduates.

Our annual SOA Watch Vigil, often called a "festival of peace and hope," grew rapidly, eventually bringing together some twenty thousand people from the United

SOA Watch attendees holding crosses. Each cross bears the name of a Latin American victim of militarism (Linda Panetta)

States, Canada, and Latin America. Those attending the vigil included many college and high school students, nuns, priests, military veterans, pacifists, families, senior citizens, union workers including Bob King, president of the United Auto Workers, celebrities Martin Sheen, Susan Sarandon, Pete Seeger, John Goodman, and others. Working very hard at the vigil was Chris Inserra of Chicago, one of the best grassroots organizers I have ever known.

Each vigil features speakers from the United States and Latin America, along with musicians and puppeteers who bring joy to all. Sunday is considered a special day, as we close our vigil with a solemn funeral procession. Thousands carry small white crosses with the names of people killed by SOA graduates; some carry photos of the victims. Over the sound system, the names of the victims and their ages, many of them children, are called. After each name is called, the thousands in the funeral procession raise the white crosses and photos and respond, "PRESENTE!" Many weep. We place the crosses and photos on the tall, locked fence at the entrance to Fort Benning.

Each year, after the solemn funeral procession has ended, there are those who, after much discernment, feel called to do a nonviolent act of civil disobedience. They go over or around the fence, carrying a cross or photo onto Fort Benning property. As they enter the military post, they are arrested, handcuffed, and charged with criminal trespass. Over the years, more than 245 people in our movement have been arrested and sent to prison —the majority getting a six-month sentence. They are called our "Prisoners of Conscience," defended pro bono by our own top-notch attorneys Peter Thompson, Bill Quigley, Bob Phares, Edward O'Sowski, and others from the SOA Watch legal collective.

Every spring, SOA Watch has brought hundreds in the movement to Washington for four days of lobbying members of Congress to cut off funding to the SOA. Among our many allies and strong supporters in Congress have been Joe Kennedy (D-MA), Joe Moakley (D-MA), Jim McGovern (D-MA), Dennis Kucinich (D-OH), and civil rights icon John Lewis (D-GA).

Documentaries and books have educated countless people about the School of the Americas, bringing thousands into the SOA Watch movement. The Maryknoll community and Jesuit priests funded the documentary *School of Assassins*, produced by Robert Richter and narrated by Susan Sarandon. The film received an Academy Award nomination. Photojournalist and filmmaker Linda Panetta produced the documentary *An Insider Speaks Out*, about Major Joseph Blair, which brought many into the movement. Blair, a former SOA instructor, retired from the Army and joined the movement to close the school. SOA Watch documentary *Somos Una America*, produced by the youth in our movement, was also a big hit.

Books that have brought many into our movement

are:

- *School of Assassins,* by Jack Nelson-Pallmeyer
- *The School of the Americas: Military Training and Political Violence,* by Lesley Gill
- *Disturbing the Peace,* by James Hodge and Linda Cooper
- *Jailed for Justice: A Women's Guide to a Federal Prison Camp,* by Clare Hanrahan
- *From Warriors to Resisters and Voices in Solidarity,* by SOA Watch Publications, edited by Margaret Knapke

Early on, a two-page article in *Newsweek* magazine by Douglas Waller, "Running a School of Dictators," advanced our cause. This was only the beginning of extensive media coverage that exposed the SOA to the general public and members of Congress. In the coming years, editorials appeared in major newspapers around the country calling for the School of the Americas to close:

- *The New York Times,* "School of the Dictators," September 28, 1996
- *The Washington Post,* "School of Scandal," October 19, 1996
- *Chicago Tribune,* "Lights Out at School of the Americas," April 16, 1999
- *Los Angeles Times,* "Bury This Relic," May 21, 1999
- *The Boston Globe,* "School of the Assassins," July 31, 1999
- *The Atlanta Constitution,* "Shut Down School of the Americas," August 4, 1999
- *Detroit Free Press,* "Torture U.," May 11, 2004

These editorials, combined with the tens of thousands of people in the SOA Watch movement and the many members of Congress calling for the school's closure, created a public relations nightmare for the Pentagon.

Aware that Congress was preparing to close the School of the Americas, the Pentagon supported a Congressional bill in January 2001 that changed the name of the school to the Western Hemisphere Institute for Security Cooperation (WHINSEC).

While we in the SOA Watch saw the name change as cosmetic, it did put the school's training courses under a microscope. The Pentagon also established a board of visitors, made up of members of Congress and others whose mission was to monitor the school's curriculum.

After the terrorist attacks on September 11, 2001, it was difficult for SOA Watch to keep Latin America on the radar screen. Shortly after 9/11, the Pentagon, in the name of national security, decided to deny public access to the names of those attending WHINSEC.

Over the years, SOA Watch has been through some challenging times, but we have always kept our hands on the plow and kept moving ahead with hope. One way we kept our hope alive was to send SOA Watch delegations to the countries that were sending troops to SOA/WHINSEC for training. We asked them to withdraw their troops.

Lisa Sullivan, our coordinator for this important project, had been a Maryknoll lay worker in Latin America for many years before joining SOA Watch. Thanks to Lisa's many contacts and hard work, our delegations were able to meet with a number of Latin American presidents. A monumental achievement for our movement was getting the presidents of Argentina, Venezuela, Ecuador, Nicaragua, and Bolivia to agree to stop sending their military personnel to SOA/WHINSEC.

SOA Watch continues to call for the closing of WHINSEC. After much discussion and discernment, however, in 2017, SOA Watch decided to hold its annual vigil at the United States/Mexico border in Nogales, Arizona. At the root of this decision was the long and brutal history of the School of the Americas. The violence caused by the more than sixty thousand SOA/WHINSEC graduates, along with gang violence, and the poverty caused by our country's economic policies, have caused thousands of people to flee their countries and come to the United States. Once again, it's about making the struggle of others "our struggle." We go to the border to express our love and solidarity with our migrant sisters and brothers. Many in SOA Watch have also joined protests around the country against the forced separation of children from their migrant parents.

I'm happy to say that our work continues, and it is a special joy to see many young people with roots in Latin America serving as leaders in the SOA Watch movement. Together we move ahead in the struggle for peace and justice in the world, always holding onto our hope.

❑

Part Two

An Injustice Closer to Home

Chapter 9

Confronting the Hypocrisy and Corruption of the All-Male Priesthood

IT WAS AN HONOR TO WORK with such good-hearted and committed people in the SOA Watch movement. In organizing our movement, we decided on a "circular" structure, one that insured all participants would have a voice, versus the hierarchical or "top-down" model with power resting solely at the top. Many of the movement's major contributors and finest leaders were women.

As a priest, I spent many years traveling extensively throughout the United States, giving talks at churches, colleges, high schools, and to peace groups about the injustice of US foreign policy in Latin America. And then, the unexpected happened. I was introduced to an injustice much closer to home. This injustice was in my church.

I began meeting devout Catholic women who told me about their calling to the Catholic priesthood. They had all been rejected by the church hierarchy because of their gender. What I heard from these women began to keep me awake at night as I asked myself some basic questions:

- Didn't our all-loving God create men and women

equal?

- Doesn't the call to be a priest come from God?
- Who are we, as men, to say that our call from God is authentic, but God's call to women is not?
- Isn't our all-powerful God who created the universe capable of empowering a woman to be a priest?

In my ministry, I also spoke with women who were not called to the priesthood, but who described to me how it felt to be a woman in the Catholic Church with words such as "inferior," "lesser," "invisible," "voiceless," and "disrespected." Some women told me that they chose to leave the church rather than remain in an "abusive relationship."

A discussion followed concerning the lifelong consequences to children who are raised in a male-dominated society. It wasn't that long ago that women could not vote, serve as members of Congress, become doctors, lawyers, pilots, astronauts, priests in the Episcopal Church or pastors in the Methodist or Presbyterian churches. Recent research (and, frankly, common sense) tells us that religious communities are not immune to the effects of patriarchy on children. We now know that girls who grow up without women religious leaders are less likely to have the same levels of self-esteem, educational attainment, and professional success as those who do. Today, girls growing up in the Catholic Church are at a clear disadvantage.

Over the years, a number of Catholic parents have confided to me that they left the church because they recognized that a male-dominated church was unhealthy for their children—both girls and boys.

One evening, following a talk, a group of Catholic women presented me with the "What is wrong with this top-down model" poster pictured above.

When the discussion ended, the women asked me to show the poster to my fellow priests, which I did. I was saddened, but not surprised, at their response. The majority were extremely upset with the poster and refused to have any discussion about our all-male priesthood. They reminded me that this was a Church teaching that was not open to debate. I shared with my fellow priests, some of them longtime friends, my growing discomfort at being in a profession that excluded women. Their response? If you don't like it, leave. Some priests told me if women became priests, that would be the day they would leave the priesthood. The response I got from my fellow priests gave me my first glimpse of the challenges ahead.

Long ago, I learned that where there is injustice, silence is complicity. What I saw in my church was a grave injustice to women, our church, and our Creator, who made women and men equal. I could not be silent.

So, wherever I spoke about the injustice of the School of the Americas, I also spoke about the injustice against women in the Catholic Church. My message got a lot of support from audiences.

There is something very liberating about confronting prejudice and seeking justice and equality. The more I studied and reflected on the reasons used to exclude women from the priesthood, the more clearly I saw that this church teaching was not of God, but of an all-male clerical culture that views women as inherently inferior to men.

It became evident that this teaching simply cannot stand up to scrutiny. It defies logic and rationality, and, frankly, it's just silly. I believe this is the reason that priests and bishops refuse to debate the issue of women priests.

In the many discussions I have had with women who want to be priests, they explained that their exclusion from the priesthood was not about theology but about power. They told me that the patriarchy that governs and dominates the Catholic Church views women as a threat to its power and status. Priests fear women, the women said, because women have the potential, if they become priests, to diminish the power and privileged lifestyle of the patriarchy.

As a member of the all-boys club for decades, I can only say that women called to the priesthood have identified what, I believe, is at the very core of this grave injustice against women in the Catholic Church. It's about power.

While most of my invitations to speak were in the United States, I was also invited to speak about the SOA at a religious conference in Rome, Italy. Hundreds of priests and nuns attended my presentation and were very supportive of our efforts to close the SOA. I regret to say that I did not address the issue of women priests in my talk.

The day before returning to the United States, I was invited by Vatican Radio to give a fifteen-minute live interview about the SOA and US foreign policy in Latin America. All went well for thirteen minutes. With two minutes remaining, I felt I could not let this sacred moment go by without expressing a few words of solidarity with women in the Church. So, I said: "I have been discussing the injustice of US foreign policy in Latin America. As a Catholic priest, in closing, I want to address an injustice closer to home—in our Church. I just want to say there will never be justice in the Catholic Church until women can be ordained."

I had another minute remaining and wanted to say something about how men dominate and claim ownership of the church, but it was not to be. The manager of Vatican Radio angrily entered the studio, cut me off the air, and started playing a Gregorian chant for the listeners. The interview was over! I was, however, very happy that my brief message about women priests was broadcast throughout Italy and other countries in Europe.

When I returned to the United States, I received a call from the head of Maryknoll saying that he had heard from the Vatican about my interview and they were very upset. It seems that I had poked the beehive of church patriarchy. I was told that what I had done was serious and against a very important Church teaching.

I continued in my many talks around the country calling for the closing of the School of the Americas—along with opening up a conversation about ordaining women in the Catholic Church. The overwhelming support I received from audiences kept my hope alive.

❑

Chapter 10

An Invitation that Changed My Life

THEN CAME AN INVITATION from Janice Sevre-Duszynska, one of the many Catholic women called to the priesthood, to attend her ordination ceremony in Lexington, Kentucky, on August 9, 2008.

Today, there are more than 300 women in ten countries who have been ordained as Catholic priests. According to the Association of Roman Catholic Women Priests (ARCWP), a validly ordained bishop, in good standing in the church, ordained the first female bishops. Therefore, the ordinations that follow are valid and within the apostolic line of succession. Still, the Vatican does not recognize these ordinations of women.

Janice Sevre-Duszynska, a schoolteacher and devout Catholic, was very active in our SOA Watch movement. After much reflection and prayer, I told Janice that it would be an honor to attend her ordination.

Hundreds attended and Bishop Dana Reynolds presided at the sacred liturgy. At the ceremony, I was invited to give a homily and said the following:

> When I met Janice Sevre-Duszynska years ago
> in the SOA Watch movement, she spoke about
> her journey of faith and her call to be a priest in

the Catholic Church. That day has arrived. Today we are here to share in her joy and to support Janice in her call to the priesthood.

As a high school teacher and person of deep faith, Janice participated in a nonviolent protest against the School of the Americas and was sent to prison for three months. Janice, as well as 230 others in the SOA Watch movement who have gone to prison, is called a "Prisoner of Conscience."

In prison, one has a lot of time for long thoughts and long prayers. Among my own thoughts as a prisoner of conscience was the issue of the ordination of women in the Catholic Church. It is my belief that we need the wisdom, experiences, compassion, and courage of women in the priesthood if our Church is to be healthy and complete.

We can go to the scriptures and find numerous passages that support the ordination of women in the Church. In Romans 16:7, we read that in the early church of Rome a woman named Junia was described by Paul as "an apostle" who was imprisoned for spreading the faith. In Galatians 3:26-28, we read, "It is through faith that you are God's sons and daughters. There is neither male nor female. In Christ you are all one." And in the Gospels, we read that after Jesus was crucified, he chose to appear first to a woman, Mary Magdalene. Jesus instructed Mary to go and bring the good news of his resurrection to the apostles who, out of fear, were hiding behind locked doors. Mary Magdalene became known as "the apostle to the apostles."

Conscience is very sacred. It gives us a sense of right and wrong and urges us to do what is right.

Conscience is what compels Janice and the other women to say, "No, we cannot deny our call from God to the priesthood." And it is our conscience that compels us to be here today. For we know that to not be here would be to participate in discrimination, which is wrong. How can we speak out against our country's foreign policy in Latin America and Iraq if we are silent about the injustice in our own Church here at home?

Janice, all of us present in this church today, and the many who cannot be here, support you and walk in solidarity with you in the struggle for peace, justice, and equality.

May our loving God bless you in your ministry and journey of faith.

The ordination of Janice was a celebration of hope and joy. But Church leaders at the Vatican, and many among my fellow priests at Maryknoll, did not share our hope and joy. Instead their response was one of anger and outrage.

When I returned to Georgia after the ceremony, I was summoned to Maryknoll headquarters in New York by the head of the Maryknoll Society (called the superior general) and members of the council. At this meeting, they asked me to explain why I attended the ordination ceremony of a woman and what the ceremony involved.

Actually, the ordination ceremony of a woman is the same as that of a man. In a personal way, I spoke briefly about the meaning and joy I found as a priest in Maryknoll, but added that now I see a problem. Hearing the stories and experiences of women, I said it troubles me to be in a profession that does not treat women as equals. I see no reason why women cannot join us as priests.

After responding to their questions and being told

that they would be sending a report of the meeting to the Vatican, I had a couple of questions for the superior general and the council members regarding women priests in the church. To my surprise, I was told there could be no discussion of women priests, citing Pope John Paul's apostolic letter of 1994, *Ordinatio Sacerdotalis*. In this document, Pope John Paul II declared that the Church has no authority to ordain women and that "this judgment is to be definitively held by all the Church's faithful." The pope concluded his letter by saying there could be no more discussion about the ordination of women in the Roman Catholic Church.

When I hear a Church leader speak like this, I am reminded of my commanding officer in Vietnam years ago who told me, "Lieutenant, your job in the military is to implement our country's foreign policy, not to question or discuss it." Today, our church leaders are saying something very similar when they tell priests and Catholics, "Your job in the church is to implement our church's teachings and not to question or discuss them."

At the meeting, I felt it was important to say that, as an adult, I find it offensive to be told that I cannot question or discuss a church teaching. I thought it important, also, to remind the council and head of Maryknoll that the issue of women priests is being discussed widely in the church—and polls are showing that the majority of Catholics support the ordination of women as priests.

At this meeting were priests who had always supported me in my ministry over the years, but now I felt I was among strangers. Without any discussion or any indication that they could support women called to be priests, the meeting ended—and their report went to the Vatican.

In the larger community of Maryknoll, there was a lot of anger at what I did. For many priests, I had done the unspeakable. For the many priests who fear women, what I had done was equivalent to joining the enemy. The few who supported me remained silent—fearful that they might get into trouble and jeopardize their power.

I returned to Georgia feeling very alone. ❑

Chapter 11

The Vatican's Response

IT DIDN'T TAKE LONG for the Vatican's letter to arrive. The letter stated that I had "caused grave scandal" in the church by participating in the ordination of a woman. Therefore, I had thirty days to recant my support for the ordination of women—or I would be expelled from the priesthood.

Because of the seriousness of the letter, I withdrew into solitude, prayer, and reflection for two weeks, after which I sent the following response to the Vatican:

November 7, 2008

TO THE CONGREGATION FOR THE DOCTRINE
OF THE FAITH, THE VATICAN

I was saddened by your letter dated October 21, 2008, giving me 30 days to recant my belief and public statements that support the ordination of women, or I will be expelled from the priest-hood.

Over the years, I have met many women in our Church who, like you and me, feel called by God to be priests. You, our Church leaders at the Vati-can, tell women they cannot be priests.

I believe what you are doing is wrong, a grave injustice, and cannot stand up to scrutiny. A 1976 report by the Vatican's Pontifical Biblical Commission supports the research of Scripture scholars, canon lawyers, and many faithful Catholics who have studied the scriptures and have concluded that there is no justification in the Bible for excluding women from the priesthood.

Women in our Church are telling us that God is calling them to the priesthood. Who are we, as men, to say to women, "Our call is valid, but yours is not"?

Hundreds of Catholic churches in the United States are closing because of a shortage of priests. Yet there are hundreds of committed and prophetic women telling us that God is calling them to serve our Church as priests. If we are to have a vibrant, healthy Church, rooted in the teachings of Jesus, we need the faith, wisdom, experience, compassion, and courage of women in the priesthood.

Conscience is very sacred. Conscience is what compelled Franz Jagerstätter, a humble Austrian farmer, husband, and father of four young children, to refuse to join Hitler's army, which led to his execution. Conscience is what compelled Rosa Parks to say she could no longer sit in the back of the bus, which led to her arrest. Conscience is what compels women in our Church to say they cannot be silent and deny their call from God to be priests. And it is my conscience that compels me to do what is right and just. I cannot and will not recant my belief and public statements that support the ordination of women in our Church.

In your letter, you stated that I "caused grave scandal" in the Catholic Church by participating in the ordination of a woman. You should know that the majority of Catholics in the United States support the ordination of women. When Catholics hear the word "scandal" they think about the thousands of children who have been raped and sexually abused by Catholic priests.

According to the newspaper *USA Today* (February 28, 2008), in the United States alone, nearly 5,000 Catholic priests have sexually abused more than 12,000 children. Many bishops, aware of these crimes, remained silent. These priests and bishops were not excommunicated. Yet the women in the Church who are called by God and ordained to serve God's people, along with priests who support them, are excommunicated.

Where there is injustice, silence is the voice of consent. Therefore, I call upon all Catholics, fellow priests, bishops, Pope Benedict, and all Church leaders at the Vatican to speak out clearly and boldly about this grave injustice being done to women in our Church.

In Peace and Justice,
Roy Bourgeois, M.M.

After mailing my letter to the Vatican, I drove seven hours to Louisiana to inform my close-knit, traditional Catholic family about my situation. Before meeting with my father (my dear mom died in 2005), I spoke with my brother and two sisters about what I had done. They were upset by what they heard and said, "You are going to break Daddy's heart."

It was a long and sleepless night.

The next day, we all gathered for our little family meeting in the old house that we all grew up in and where my elderly father still lived. I began with a short prayer before giving each family member a copy of the letter I had sent the Vatican. I went outside while they read the letter, and I prayed that somehow they would understand what I was doing.

Like most families I know, we had been through some difficult times together. Over the years, I had always felt grateful for the love and support I received from my parents and siblings.

When I volunteered to go to war in Vietnam, they were upset, yet they wrote loving letters to me often and sent hundreds of packages for the children in the orphanage. When I was ordained and went to work with the poor of Bolivia, they wondered why I hadn't chosen to work with the poor of the United States. Yet, during my five years in Bolivia, they wrote often and organized raffles and football pools in our little town to raise money for the poor of La Paz. (My mom was a great organizer.)

And like most people I know, they had a hard time understanding civil disobedience and going off to prison for one's beliefs. Yet they came to my trials and visited me in prison.

Waiting outside on the porch as they read my letter, I realized that my going against the Catholic Church's teaching was going to be the biggest challenge ever for my family. I was preparing myself for the worst.

I went back inside the house and asked what they thought of my letter. I was hoping that my two sisters or brother would begin by expressing some support for me, which would help bring my dad on board. Instead, my younger sister asked my dad what he thought about the letter.

My father was a religious, soft-hearted, kind, and loving person. He didn't say anything. He began to cry. When he regained his composure, he said, "God brought Roy back from Vietnam and took care of him in Bolivia and in prison. God is going to take care of him now. Roy is doing the right thing, and I support him." He stood up, came over, and gave me a hug. My brother and two sisters joined us with hugs and tears.

I had worried so much about my family's reaction to what I had done that it was hard to believe their loving response. I felt as if a boulder had been lifted off my back, and I was filled with indescribable joy and peace. My dad's blessing brought my siblings and a number of my nieces and nephews into the women's ordination issue. As one of my nieces put it, "Uncle Roy, how can the Vatican tell you to go against your conscience? Don't they know that this would be a lie, and lying is a sin?"

I returned to Georgia feeling a deep inner peace and awaited a response to my letter. Leaving my little town, I drove by the high school I had attended many years earlier when it was segregated. I couldn't help but think about how, in our ignorance and lack of faith, we tried to justify our prejudice toward others. When it came to racism, the mantras were "segregation is our tradition" and we are "separate but equal."

On the long drive back to Georgia, I thought about how the patriarchy of the Catholic Church is doing the exact same thing to women in the church. They claim that the all-male priesthood is "our tradition" and that "men and women are equal, but have different roles."

Let's face it! Sexism, like racism, is a sin. And no matter how hard we may try to justify our discrimination against others, it is not the way of our all-loving God who made everyone of equal worth and dignity. Sorry, there are no exceptions.

❏

Chapter 12

Response from Maryknoll

A S THE MONTHS UNFOLDED, I continued to travel, giving talks around the country about the School of the Americas—and gender equality in the Catholic Church. Meanwhile, my Maryknoll community and the Canon lawyers I had consulted assured me that I was still a priest and a member of Maryknoll. Therefore, I continued in my ministry.

Then, on March 18, 2011, a little more than two years after I had received the Vatican's letter insisting that I recant my support for women priests, a certified letter arrived from the superior general of the Maryknoll Society. His letter stated that my continued support for the ordination of women was "causing grave scandal to the people of God, the Church, especially in the United States, and many of the Maryknoll priests and Brothers." The letter concluded by saying that if I did not recant my support for the ordination of women within fifteen days, I would be expelled from the Maryknoll community.

Once again, I refused to recant.

On July 27, 2011, Maryknoll's superior general sent me a "Second and Final Canonical Warning," giving me fifteen days to recant or he would proceed with the process of my dismissal from Maryknoll and the priesthood.

Again, he brought up the "grave scandal" I was causing in the Catholic Church and among members of the Maryknoll community.

In response, on August 8, 2011, I sent the following letter to the superior general and all the members of Maryknoll in the United States, Latin America, Africa, and Asia:

TO THE SUPERIOR GENERAL
AND ALL MEMBERS OF MARYKNOLL

My Brothers,

I have been a Catholic priest for 39 years and Maryknoll has been my faith community, my family, during these years. So, it was with great sadness that I received the letter (Second and Final Canonical Warning) from the Superior General, dated July 27, 2011, stating that I must recant my belief and public statements that support the ordination of women or I will be dismissed from Maryknoll.

In my ministry, I have met many devout women in our Church who believe God is calling them to be priests. Why wouldn't they be called? God created men and women of equal worth and dignity and, as we all know, the call to be a priest comes from God.

My brothers, who are we to reject God's call of women to the priesthood? The Holy Scriptures remind us in Galatians 3:28, "There is neither male nor female. In Christ you are one." How is it possible for us to say that our call from God, as men, is authentic, but God's call of women is not?

After much reflection, study, and prayer, I believe that our Church's teaching that excludes women from the priesthood defies both faith and reason and cannot stand up to scrutiny. This teaching has nothing to do with God, but with men, and is rooted in sexism. Sexism, like racism, is a sin. And no matter how hard we may try to justify discrimination against women, in the end, it is not the way of God, but of men, who want to hold on to their power.

As people of faith, we believe in the primacy of conscience. Our conscience connects us to the Divine. Our conscience gives us a sense of right and wrong and urges us to do what is right, what is just.

What I am being asked to do is not possible without betraying my conscience. In essence, you are telling me to lie and say I do not believe that God calls both men and women to the priesthood. This I cannot do; therefore, I will not recant.

I firmly believe that the exclusion of women from the priesthood is a grave injustice against women, against our Church, and against God.

As you know, I am not a lone voice crying out in the wilderness for the ordination of women. Polls show that the majority of Catholics support having women as their priests. Many fellow priests tell me they believe women should be ordained, but these brothers are afraid to break their silence because of the consequences.

Many years ago, as a young man in the military, I felt God was calling me to be a priest. I entered Maryknoll and found the happiness, meaning, and hope I was seeking in life by following my call. Why should we deny this call from God—this gift from God—to women?

My brothers, in God's eyes there is neither male nor female. We are one. Just as you and I were called to be priests by our loving God, women are also being called to serve our Church as priests. Let us welcome them and give thanks to God.

Your brother in Christ,
Roy Bourgeois, M.M.

Months passed and, as with the letter I sent to the

Vatican, I did not receive a response from the superior general of Maryknoll. I did, however, receive many personal responses from members of Maryknoll in the United States, Latin America, Africa, and Asia. While the majority of the letters were kind and supported me in my work in the SOA Watch movement, not one priest said that he supported the ordination of women in the church. Dr. Martin Luther King Jr. was right when he said, "In the end, we will remember not the words of our enemies, but the silence of our friends."

❑

Chapter 13

A Sign of Hope

A SIGN OF HOPE CAME when I attended the annual meeting of all Maryknoll Society members working in the United States, at the Maryknoll Society Center in Ossining, New York.

On the second day of the three-day meeting, I was invited to address the community about why I was supporting the ordination of women. In attendance were longtime priest friends who had always supported me in my ministry. I spoke for fifteen minutes and then invited comments and questions. At all my other talks at churches and colleges and with peace groups around the country, I received great support in my advocacy for women priests. In my own community, it was quite different. My fellow priests could not get beyond why I was going against a Church teaching and how I could be disobedient to the pope and our Maryknoll superior general, who were telling me to be silent. A number of priests were angry because my support of women's ordination caused some donors to stop contributing to Maryknoll. Of all of the talks I've ever given, this was the most difficult and frustrating. Another sleepless night followed.

The next day, the senior members of the community,

including two former superiors general of Maryknoll, asked me to meet with them. At the meeting, they asked what they could do to help me in the serious situation I was in with the Vatican and Maryknoll. I appreciated their question and concern. I responded by saying that I was not the issue, but rather the way women are treated in our church: They do not have a voice or any power. They are invisible. I asked if they would be willing to write a short statement in support of gender equality and the ordination of women in our church, sign it, and send it to the Vatican and the superior general of Maryknoll. I also asked that they encourage other members of Maryknoll to sign on to the letter. I mentioned that the Vatican and Maryknoll would be hesitant to expel a large number of priests, knowing that most Catholics support the ordination of women. In closing, I told them that this issue was not complicated. It was about justice, equality, and solidarity.

There was silence. After a brief discussion, with no mention of women priests, the meeting ended. Once again, I returned to Georgia feeling very alone.

As a result of our meeting, a couple weeks later they sent me a copy of the letter they sent to the superior general of Maryknoll and members of the council. It was signed by fifty-one Maryknoll priests, including five former superiors general of Maryknoll. The letter, dated August 11, 2011, stated:

TO THE SUPERIOR GENERAL OF MARYKNOLL
AND MEMBERS OF THE COUNCIL

In recent months, you and Maryknoll as a whole have struggled to understand the complex matters surrounding our brother, Roy Bourgeois. For more than four decades, Roy has been our brother and served the mission of the Catholic

Church. We are aware that there are issues involving Roy with which some of his brother Maryknollers strongly agree while others strongly disagree. We are also very much aware of the responsibilities of leadership that weigh heavily upon you.

As missionary priests and brothers, we have first and foremost dedicated our lives to proclaiming the Gospel of Jesus Christ while living together at the common table. This faith and commitment to Maryknoll now calls us to break our silence. We, the undersigned, are asking that you not dismiss Roy Bourgeois from Maryknoll. We also ask that you slow down the process in order to engage Society members in further reflection together on this issue. It is a matter that touches all of us, and we have the right to be brought into the loop. We are looking for an open and prayerful discernment regarding our brother. We truly want to be involved.

You are daily in our prayers,

[Signed by fifty-one members of the Maryknoll community]

There was no mention of the ordination of women in the letter. This letter from my fellow priests was quite different from an earlier letter from women in the National Coalition of American Nuns, signed by 113 nuns, including Sister Joan Chittister, OSB. Their letter, which generated a lot of media coverage, read:

Cardinal William Joseph Levada
Congregation for the Doctrine of the Faith
The Vatican

Dear Cardinal Levada,

The Vatican's threatened excommunication of Fr. Roy Bourgeois because of his belief in the priestly ordination of women has diminished our Church.

As women religious who love our Church and who have served the People of God for decades, we support our brother Roy. As a Maryknoll priest for 36 years, he has followed the Gospel of Jesus in his ministry for peace and justice by speaking out against the war in Iraq and against the torture of countless human beings, aided and abetted by the U.S. government's School of the Americas. He has been a prophetic voice for thousands in our society.

Roy is now a prophetic voice in our Church because of his support for women's equality in all Church ministries. Excommunications depend not on edicts or laws, but on compliance. We do not believe Roy is outside the community and we embrace him wholeheartedly. Like Roy, we know women who testify that they are called to priesthood. We know that Jesus did not discriminate in calling both women and men to ministry. And we know that our Church needs the gifts of everyone called.

So, we join Fr. Roy Bourgeois and the majority of U.S. Catholics, who believe that women are called to priestly ordination in the Catholic Church. We look forward to the day when Catholic women, following in the footsteps of Mary Magdalene who announced the Resurrection to the male Apostles, will minister as full equals in our Church.

Sincerely,

[Signed by 113 nuns]

International delegation advocating women's ordination in St. Peter's Square, Vatican City, October 2011. Back row (l-r): Therese Koturbash; Nicole Sotelo; Mike Toner; Bob Heineman; Miriam Duignan; Jeannette Mulherin; Bill Quigley; Debbie Dupre Quigley; Kate Conmy; Fr. Roy Bourgeois, M.M.; Dorothy Irvin; Pat McSweeney. Front row: Erin Saiz Hanna; Donna Rougeux; Janice Sevre-Duszynska; Ree Hudson

In October of 2011, I was invited to join the Women's Ordination Conference (WOC) delegation of women's ordination leaders going to the Vatican. There we met with a few church leaders and delivered a petition signed by fifteen thousand supporters of women's ordination. Most church leaders refused to meet with our delegation. We also showed the documentary film *Pink Smoke over the Vatican* at a nearby theater. This award-winning film, produced in the United States by Jules Hart, presents the powerful voices of women who are the vanguard of the women's ordination movement. While the showing was well attended, not one priest or bishop from the Vatican attended. The majority of priests in the United States have also refused to see this award-winning documentary.

Our delegation held a vigil in Saint Peter's Square, holding banners that said ORDAIN CATHOLIC WOMEN and GOD IS CALLING WOMEN TO BE PRIESTS. Italian

International delegation advocating women's ordination
in Saint Peter's Square, Vatican City, October 2011

police confiscated our banners and detained members of
the delegation for three hours. Once again, we had
poked the beehive of church patriarchy. I returned to my
ministry in the United States feeling more hopeful in the
struggle for equality.

While I continued to be disappointed by the lack of
support from my fellow priests, I was encouraged by
Catholics in the pews. The Vatican and the head of
Maryknoll, along with most priests, continued to refer to
women priests as "a grave scandal in the church."

❏

Chapter 14

Sexual Abuse Scandal

ON FEBRUARY 28, 2008, the national newspaper *USA Today* reported that in the United States alone, nearly five thousand Catholic priests had sexually abused more than twelve thousand children.

In 2010, the Vatican caused an uproar when it announced that the ordination of women as priests is a crime comparable to that of the sexual abuse of children.

More recently, scandal once again rocked the Catholic Church. This time, it's six Catholic dioceses in Pennsylvania. According to a grand jury report released on August 14, 2018, beginning in the 1950s more than three hundred "predator priests" sexually abused more than one thousand children. The grand jury believed "the real number of abused children might be in the thousands" since some records were lost and victims were afraid to come forward.

"The main thing was not to help children, but to avoid scandal," the report said. "Priests were raping little boys and girls, and the men of God who were responsible for them not only did nothing; they hid it all. For decades."

The 1,400–page report, written by twenty-three

grand jurors over the course of two years, describes the horrific crimes of Catholic priests:

- In Erie, a seven-year-old boy was sexually abused by a priest who told him he should go to confession and confess his "sins" to that same priest.
- In the Pittsburgh diocese, "a ring of predatory priests shared information regarding victims, as well as exchanging the victims amongst themselves. The ring manufactured child pornography and used whips, violence, and sadism in raping the victims."
- One priest abused five sisters in the same family, including one girl beginning when she was eighteen months old.
- Another priest was allowed to stay in ministry after impregnating a young girl and arranging for her to have an abortion.
- A priest raped a seven-year-old girl in her hospital room after a tonsillectomy. What was his punishment? The Vatican's Congregation for the Doctrine of the Faith decided, after reviewing his crime, that he should remain a priest and "live a life of prayer and penance."

It's important to note that among the thousands of Catholic priests who raped and sexually abused thousands of children, the vast majority were not expelled from the priesthood or excommunicated. Every woman who has been ordained as a priest in the Catholic Church has been expelled and excommunicated by the Vatican.

The grand jury report stated that the Catholic hierarchy "protected their institution at all costs and maintained strategies to avoid scandal." Victims were discouraged from going to the police. Priests who got in trouble in one diocese were shuffled to another diocese, where they abused other children. Church officials followed a "playbook for concealing the truth," minimizing the abuse by using words like "inappropriate contact" or "boundary issues" instead of "rape." In one case, a priest's repeated and violent sexual assaults of children were referred to as "his difficulties."

According to the Database of Accused U.S. Clergy available at BishopAccountability.org, the number of accused U.S. clergy topped 7,300 on September 15, 2021. Also, twenty-six Catholic dioceses and three religious orders have filed for bankruptcy protection because of the clergy sexual abuse scandal.

In the midst of all the corruption, evil, and crimes committed by so many Catholic priests and bishops, I cannot help but believe that, if the Catholic Church had women priests and married priests, the Church would not be in the crisis it is in today. There is no hope or future in an all-male priesthood.

In March of 2013, a *New York Times*/CBS News poll revealed that 70 percent of US Catholics believe that Pope Francis should let women be priests.

❑

Chapter 15

More Signs of Hope

ENTERING 2012, I still had not heard anything from the Vatican or the head of the Maryknoll Society. No news was good news, I felt. I continued in my ministry and was filled with renewed hope as I began receiving hundreds of letters and emails from people around the country who supported women's ordination. The following is a sampling of their messages.

From a Catholic mother of four:

Many of our churches are closing because of a shortage of priests. Considering half the planet is female, the solution is quite obvious. But no, we would rather close churches than even discuss the ordination of women.

Christ surrounded himself with both faithful men and women, but the women were simply written out of history by those who recorded it all: the men.

One by one, I had to explain to my three daughters why they could not be considered for the priesthood. Ludicrous but true, they were missing body parts with which their brother had been bestowed. This is ignorance at its worst.

From a Catholic father of four daughters:

I am writing to you as a lifetime Catholic. My wife and I have raised four bright, sensitive, and compassionate daughters, none of whom attend the Catholic Church any longer.

I have seen firsthand, through my daughters, how they have been discriminated against by sexist language, an all-male clergy, and being excluded from the diaconate and priesthood.

I am a dad who is hurting because I see how my daughters have suffered because of sexism in our Church.

From a deacon in the Catholic Church:

I was called in by the bishop because of my sermon that expressed support for women priests in our Church.

During the discussion I told the bishop I had two daughters, and if God calls them to be priests, I will support them in their call. The bishop looked at me and said, "Don't worry, God will not call them." I left the meeting thinking, "What arrogance!"

This letter reminded me of the question I had been asking many of my fellow priests: "If your sister told you that she, like you, were being called by God to the priesthood, would you support her?" The majority of them said they would not support her because it went against the church's teaching that only males can be priests.

From a college student:

The pope tells us that women cannot be priests because Jesus chose only male apostles. Doesn't he realize that a woman was chosen to bring Jesus into this world, and that without Mary there wouldn't be a Jesus? As a Catholic, I've always seen Mary as the first priest. Who is more qualified to say the words that male priests say at Mass? "This is My Body. This is My Blood."

From a longtime Catholic:
As a young girl I was really looking forward to being an altar server in our Church. But when this new priest became the pastor, he stopped girls from being altar servers. My brother, who was an altar server, resigned the next day. This was my first experience of solidarity.

As my work continued, I experienced a real expression of solidarity from a well-known, highly respected Catholic seminary. On May 12, 2012, I received an honorary degree of Doctor of Divinity from Chicago Theological Seminary at the University of Chicago. The citation affirmed my work in the School of Americas Watch and went on to state:

Over the years, Father Bourgeois has also worked closely with many women whose courageous struggle for human rights was also accompanied by advocacy for opening the priesthood of the Roman Catholic Church to women as well as men. Just as silence over our complicity in the violation of human rights in Latin America was not possible, so too, silence in the face of the denial of the full participation of women in the ministry and leadership of the Church became impossible. While his relationship to his religious superiors and church hierarchy has often been marked by mutual respect, the prophetic voice often disturbs those who wield institutional privilege. Just as his willingness to break civil law for the sake of the Gospel often led him to a Federal Courthouse in Georgia, his readiness in recent years to challenge church law barring women from the priesthood has led to proceedings for dismissal from the Maryknoll Order and to a pending tribunal in Rome.

Because he is a conduit of divine grace, a tireless worker for justice, a prophet of a future not his own, Chicago Theological Seminary confers upon Father Roy Bourgeois the honorary degree of Doctor of Divinity.

It's worth noting that this is the seminary Maryknollers now attend during their preparation for the priesthood.

In contrast to that encouragement, some of the letters I received from fellow priests kept me humble. A few excerpts:

From a Roman Catholic priest in Rome:
You should apologize to the Vatican and to Maryknoll for all the scandal you are causing in our Holy Church.

From a Roman Catholic priest in Wisconsin:
"Why don't you just leave the Catholic Church and join one of the many other churches that ordain women?"

From a fellow Maryknoll priest:
I pray that you take the heroic step and recant your statements that support the ordination of women. The Catholic Church has spoken and it is your duty to obey and submit. This is what every Catholic, and especially every priest, must do. Our

conscience can never go against the official teaching of the Catholic Church. Put your conscience aside and submit to the Pope.

❏

Chapter 16

From Hope to Despair

ON OCTOBER 4, 2012, the letter from the Vatican's Congregation for the Doctrine of the Faith arrived. The letter stated that Pope Benedict XVI had canonically dismissed me from the priesthood because of my refusal to recant my support for the ordination of women in the Catholic Church.

I must say, I thought that after a long and difficult struggle, I would have been prepared for such a response from the Vatican and Pope Benedict. I wasn't.

Being expelled from the priesthood and my Maryknoll community of longtime friends after forty years was much more difficult than I had anticipated. Never before had I experienced such hurt and rejection. I wept and felt a real need to just be alone in my sadness.

Close friends, a few who had been through painful divorces, told me that healing would come, but it would be a very long and difficult journey. They were right!

I had to deal with a lot of anger and disappointment toward my fellow priests, especially those who were close friends. Not one of them was willing to join me in calling for the ordination of women. While a few told me in private that they believed women should be priests, their fear of going public kept them silent. The majority of my fellow priests, however, vehemently opposed the ordination of women and were angry at my support for women called to priesthood. They were not even willing to discuss the issue. They believed, as Pope John Paul II had said in 1994, there could be no more discussion about it.

I couldn't help but think about Galileo, the astronomer and physicist who was silenced by the Vatican in the fifteenth century for his claim that planet Earth was not the center of the universe. Galileo said, "I do not feel obliged to believe that the same God who has endowed us with senses, reason, and intellect has intended us to forgo their use."

And with my fellow priests refusing to even discuss the issue of women priests, I thought about Saint Paul's First Letter to the Corinthians (1 Cor. 13:11), which said: "When I was a child I thought like a child, talked like a child and acted like a child. But now I am an adult and have no use for childish ways."

It saddens me to say that the majority of priests I know have never grown up and become adults. Their blind obedience to authority and church teaching, along with their fear of being punished and losing their power and status in the church, prevent them from using, as Galileo said, the senses, reason, and intellect God gave us.

Over the years in my many talks at churches and colleges and to peace groups around the country, I always emphasized the importance of holding on to hope and joy in life and not allowing our anger to dominate us. I often mentioned the "joy attacks" I would get in my ministry and work in the SOA Watch.

After being kicked out of the priesthood and my Maryknoll community, however, I must confess that my anger began to dominate me. Longtime friends confronted me about this and started asking about what had happened to that hope and joy I always talked about.

One of my friends sent me the statement Nelson Mandela made when he left prison in South Africa after spending twenty-seven years there because of his resistance against racism. He said, "As I walked out of prison toward a gate that would lead me to freedom, I knew if I didn't leave my bitterness and anger behind, I'd still be in prison."

These words of Nelson Mandela were a great gift to me, for I began to realize that if I did not let go of the anger I felt toward my fellow priests, I too would be imprisoned.

❏

Chapter 17

Rediscovering Hope and Joy

I'M HAPPY TO SAY that after a long and hard struggle, I'm finally beginning to experience the peace, joy, and hope I once had in my life. The other day I even had one of those "joy attacks." But I must admit that where I find my hope has changed. I no longer find hope in the members of the all-male priesthood. Their addiction to power and fear of women is so deep that they are incapable of change. Among the more than 30,000 Catholic priests in the United States, I know of only three who are publicly calling for the ordination of women. I did get two priest friends to agree to wear an ORDAIN WOMEN button in their coffins. They said, "What can they do to me now?"

In 1975, the Women's Ordination Conference (WOC) was founded. Years later, Roman Catholic Women Priests (RCWP) and the Association of Roman Catholic Women Priests (ARCWP) came into being. Since 1975, these women have attempted dialogue with priests and bishops about women's call to priesthood. These clergy have refused to meet with the women.

I've heard women in WOC, RCWP, and ARCWP, along with LGBTQ Catholics, describe priests and bishops as "bullies." Bullies, as we all know, abuse their power and beat up on people. I knew bullies in high school, college, and the military, and it saddens me to say that I know many priest and bishop bullies in the church. No one likes a bully.

Pink Smoke over the Vatican is an award-winning documentary about the women priest movement in the Catholic Church. When it was released, I sent a copy to Pope Francis, more than three hundred Catholic bishops in the United States and hundreds of priests. Only five bishops and a dozen priests acknowledged that they received the documentary. Seven said they would watch it.

Years ago, while I was living under a dictatorship in Bolivia, the oppressed people of the country told me that change would not come from the oppressors but from the oppressed, not from the top down but from the bottom up. They said that oppressors had become enslaved by their power and would not, out of the goodness of their hearts, relinquish that power and wealth.

What they said about oppressors in Latin America can be applied to the patriarchy that dominates and claims ownership of the Catholic Church. These men in the all-male priesthood will not, in the name of justice or out of the goodness of their hearts, relinquish their power and status for women they view as inferior. Nor will it come from the CEO of the patriarchy, the pope.

I was expelled from the priesthood and Maryknoll by Pope Benedict just four months before Pope Francis was elected. I always thought that had Pope Francis been in office at the time, I would not have been expelled. I was wrong. In 2016, Pope Francis announced that on the issue of having women priests in the church, he agreed with Pope John Paul II. The door is closed. Women cannot be priests.

I find great hope and joy in knowing that men, no matter how hard they work at it, cannot keep doors closed forever. For many years, men kept the door closed on a woman's right to vote and her ability to become a medical doctor, lawyer, or member of Congress.

I have no doubt that the Catholic Church will one day open the door and welcome women into the priesthood. If it does not, it will go the way of the dinosaurs.

What Maryknoll is experiencing today is but a microcosm of what is going on throughout the Roman Catholic Church.

When I entered Maryknoll in 1966, there were over 300 seminarians and over 1,000 priests in the community. Today, there are eighteen seminarians and 252 priests and Brothers. Of these 252, 204 are over seventy years old.

The Maryknoll seminary building in Ossining is now closed and has become a retirement home for the elderly priests.

In 2020, Maryknoll ordained one priest. In 2020, twenty-five priests died.

Because of such a shortage of priests, Maryknoll has been forced to close many of its ministries serving the poor in Latin America, Asia, and Africa.

During my forty years as a priest, hundreds of priests in my Maryknoll community, many of them good friends, fell in love and married. They were all forced to leave the priesthood.

Somehow, I cannot picture Jesus telling one of his followers that he had to leave the faith community because he fell in love and got married. Madness! Ignorance at its worst! This is but another example of what the patriarchy of the Catholic Church thinks of women.

Catholicism is in a crisis throughout the world. An article by Jason Horowitz in the *New York Times* (May 27, 2018) stated:

- Only one in five Catholics attend Mass in Spain. In

France, it's one in ten. In the Netherlands, Mass attendance is down to about 5 percent. In Germany, financial contributions to the Church have thinned.

- In Ireland, this week's vote that legalized abortion was only the latest leap away from a Church that long dominated the country's culture. Ireland had already voted to legalize gay marriage.

- In mostly Catholic Luxembourg, the government, led by a gay prime minister, abolished religious teaching in state schools in September. In 2012, the Archdiocese of Vienna consolidated its 660 parishes into 150.

- In Brazil, which has the world's largest Catholic population, evangelicals preaching a prosperity gospel are giving stiff competition to Catholicism, which is projected to become a minority faith in 2030.

This crisis in the Catholic Church is not complicated. If the patriarchy that dominates the church is not dismantled and women are not treated as equals, the church will continue to diminish and, eventually, die.

In the ongoing struggle for justice and equality in the Catholic Church, my hope is in women and youth. I am grateful for the women in the church who have educated and empowered me to break my silence about the hypocrisy and corruption of the all-male priesthood. And I am grateful to our young people, including in my own family, who refuse to belong to any church or organization that does not treat all of its members as equals. My hope was stronger than ever when I attended the Women's

March in Washington, DC, on January 21, 2017. More than five hundred thousand attended.

❏

Women's March, Washington, DC, January 21, 2017

Chapter 18

Confronting the Ignorance, Cruelty, and Heresy of the Catholic Church's Teaching on Homosexuality

*"Men never do evil so completely and cheerfully
as when they do it from religious conviction."*
— Blaise Pascal

AFTER BEING KICKED OUT of Maryknoll and the priesthood, I received many invitations to speak around the country about women's ordination in the Catholic Church.

After one talk, I was approached by Catholic parents who asked me if we could meet in private. In our meeting, they told me about their high school–aged son who was gay. While they were loving and accepting of their son's sexual orientation, he was bullied at school and hurt deeply by things their priest had said at Mass about gay people. Two weeks before graduation, their son committed suicide. In their sadness and sorrow, they told me something I will never forget. They told me that they had left the Catholic Church because they were convinced that the church's teaching on homosexuality had contributed to their son's death.

A couple of weeks later, I went on an SOA Watch delegation to El Salvador. Among our many meetings with human rights and government leaders, we also met with members of the LGBTQ community. They told us about the danger of coming out in El Salvador and how many of their close friends had been killed for being gay. El Salvador is a very Catholic country. When I asked what kind of support they were getting from the Church, they said that Catholic bishops and priests were their biggest enemies.

As the months unfolded, I continued to hear stories about what LGBTQ people were experiencing. What I heard only confirmed what a growing number of people understand: As human beings, we do not choose our race, gender, sexual orientation, or gender identity. Life is a sacred gift from an all-loving God who created every-one of equal worth and dignity. There are no exceptions!

When we look at the Catholic Church's teaching on homosexuality, we find a very serious problem. The official teaching, as stated by the Catechism of the Catholic Church, Section 2357–2358, states that homosexuality is an "objective disorder." This teaching implies that our all-loving Creator made a mistake when it comes to the millions of LGBTQ people in our world. This is theology at its worst—a church teaching rooted in ignorance and heresy.

For many LGBTQ people, this teaching instills shame, self-hatred, and rejection. It has contributed to gay people being expelled from their families, fired from their jobs, bullied, and even killed. This teaching also contributes to the high rate of suicide, especially among LGBTQ teenagers.

Homophobia, according to *Webster's* dictionary, is "the irrational hatred or fear of homosexuals." The church's actions and language breed hatred and fear and often cause untold suffering and death to our LGBTQ sisters and brothers. The time has arrived for people of faith and goodwill to rid our world of homophobia.

Addressing the Catholic Church's teaching on homosexuality and the church's leaders who support this cruel and antiquated teaching is a good place to start.

Women's March, Washington, DC, January 21, 2017

Catholics welcomed the pope's words, "Who am I to judge?" However, according to *America* magazine, December 7, 2016, Pope Francis also said that he agrees with Pope Benedict that "persons with homosexual tendencies" should not be admitted to Catholic seminaries.

Moreover, on May 24, 2018, Reuters reported from Vatican City that Pope Francis, in a closed-door meeting with Italian bishops, affirmed an existing Vatican ban on gay men entering the priesthood. Reuters reported Pope Francis as saying: "Keep an eye on the admissions to seminaries, keep your eyes open. If in doubt, better not to let them [gay men] enter."

Sexism and homophobia are not the way of God, yet they are condoned by the patriarchy of the Catholic Church.

It is time for Pope Francis, as the spiritual leader of the Catholic Church, to exercise his power and change this man-made teaching that does not reflect the dignity and sacredness of God's LGBTQ sons and daughters.

It is important to point out that many priests are gay, including many bishops and cardinals. In Maryknoll, gay priests are treated with dignity and respect. Some are in leadership positions in the community. But they know that there are conditions. As gay priests, they are not permitted to question or speak out against the church's teaching on homosexuality.

Not long after my expulsion from Maryknoll and the priesthood, I wrote a letter to a number of gay priests in Maryknoll, who had been longtime friends. In my letter, I shared with them my meeting with the Catholic parents whose gay son had committed suicide and that they felt the church's teaching on homosexuality had contributed to his death. I also mentioned the plight of gay people in El Salvador and how they are persecuted by Catholic priests and bishops.

Reminding them of the power and voice they have as Catholic priests, I asked if they would consider expressing some support for LGBTQ people, especially the vulnerable young people, who are powerless and voiceless.

Not one responded to my letter. This did not surprise me. They know very well that if they break their silence about the church's teaching to express their solidarity with the LGBTQ community, they will anger the patriarchy and jeopardize their power and many privileges.

I find it very sad that there are no limits to the abuse some people will tolerate in order to hold on to power—including being labeled "disordered." Worth noting, I've been told by gay priests that most bishops and priests who aggressively attack gay people are themselves gay.

I'm happy to say that most people today view homosexuality quite differently from the Catholic Church's patriarchy:

- ·In 1973, the American Psychiatric Association declared that homosexuality is a normal variation of human sexuality.

- ·In 1976, the American Psychological Association passed a resolution that stated, "Homosexuality is not a mental disorder."
- ·Tim Cook, CEO of Apple, said, "I'm proud to be gay, and I consider being gay among the greatest gifts God has given me."
- ·In South Africa, Bishop Desmond Tutu, recipient of the Nobel Peace Prize, said, "I would not worship a God who is homophobic, and that is how deeply I feel about this. I am as passionate about this as I ever was about apartheid. For me, it is at the same level."
- ·In 2003, the Episcopal Church in the United States ordained its first openly gay bishop and in 2015 began performing same-sex marriage.
- ·On June 26, 2015, the US Supreme Court ruled that same-sex marriage is a constitutional right.
- ·On November 16, 2015, Catholic Ireland passed a law, by popular vote, which made same-sex marriage legal.
- ·A Pew Research Center survey, on December 23, 2015, reported: "A majority of US Christians now say that homosexuality should be accepted, rather than discouraged by society, including 70 percent of Catholics and 66 percent of mainline Protestants."

While there have been tremendous strides made in the struggle for LGBTQ equality, there is still much work to be done:

- ·"Nearly two-thirds of LGBTQ Americans report having experienced discrimination in their personal lives," the Human Rights Campaign says, and "only nineteen states explicitly prohibit discrimination based on sexual orientation."

- ·While twenty-five countries have legalized same-sex marriage, seventy-five nations treat homosexual behavior as a crime. In ten countries, it is punishable by death. According to Time magazine, August 17, 2015, Uganda introduced a bill in 2009 calling for the death penalty for gay people. Minister of Ethics and Integrity Simon Lokodo, a Catholic priest, supported this bill, which was passed in 2013. In 2014, it was overturned on a technicality.

Bondings, a publication of New Ways Ministry, reported on May 16, 2017, that "The list of painful actions Catholic institutions have been taking against LGBTQ people is staggering. LGBTQ people are fired from church jobs, denied sacraments or liturgical participation at funerals of family members, and perhaps the most emotionally painful action, children of LGBTQ people are denied entrance into Catholic schools."

❑

Chapter 19

The Truth Cannot be Silenced

THESE ARE CHALLENGING TIMES for the many people around the world working for equality. There are days when I have difficulty finding hope in the struggle.

I've learned, however, that we can often find hope in the most unexpected places. While writing this book, there were times when I got discouraged. Needing a break, I decided to go to the Vatican Embassy in Washington, DC, for a few days to hold a silent vigil. Each day, I stood alone in front of the embassy and alternated my use of two banners: ORDAIN WOMEN and CATHO-LIC CHURCH: STOP PERSECUTING LGBTQ PEOPLE.

The embassy is located on Massachusetts Avenue, with a wide sidewalk and constant traffic that frequently stops for a traffic light in front of the five-story building.

Over the years, I've protested with hundreds, some-times thousands of people, when passersby might be hesitant to stop to interact. Standing alone as a "solitary witness" is a unique experience. Being alone makes a person less intimidating and therefore more approach-able.

People walking down the sidewalk or on their bicy-cles would often stop to talk and share their beliefs. Most who stopped agreed with the messages on the banners. Many people passing in cars would honk and give me a thumbs-up, some pulling over to talk. It was a special joy when parents with their children stopped. I was quite surprised when a few priests who worked at the embassy came out to visit. While polite, they did not agree with my messages—but they did agree to take my flyer.

At the end of each day, I was tired from standing, but felt energized and joyful from all the support I had received from strangers. I returned to Georgia with my hope renewed.

Then came the COVID-19 pandemic that prevented us from traveling, giving talks, and protesting as before.

A group of us decided to launch a national billboard campaign calling for the ordination of women in the Catholic Church.

The billboard went up in the following cities and was seen by tens of thousands of people: New Orleans, LA; Lafayette, LA; South Bend, IN (near Notre Dame); Pittsburgh, PA; Syracuse, NY; Buffalo, NY; Milwaukee, WI; and Lincoln, NE.

For more information on the billboard campaign, see facebook.com/groups/equalrites.

We also published this ad (next page) in newspapers of the following Catholic universities: Notre Dame,

Boston College, Loyola University Chicago, and Marquette University, along with ads placed in a number of secular newspapers.

STOP MALE SUPREMACY IN THE CATHOLIC CHURCH! ORDAIN WOMEN PRIESTS!

After serving as a Catholic priest for 40 years, I was expelled from the priesthood because of my public support for the ordination of women.

An all-loving God created women and men of equal worth and dignity and called both to be priests.

Excluding women from the priesthood is no different than when women could not vote or be medical doctors, lawyers or members of congress.

In Equality,

Roy Bourgeois

For more information:
www.roybourgeoisjourney.org
https://www.facebook.com/groups/equalrites

Where there is injustice, silence is consent. In closing, I want to thank the many people who empowered me to break my silence about the grave injustice of male supremacy in the Catholic Church.

I don't know what can be more important than working for equality in society and in our faith communities. In this struggle, we can all do something.

❏

Resources

Websites for More Information

Women's Ordination Conference
womensordination.org

Roman Catholic Womenpriests
romancatholicwomenpriests.org

Association of Roman Catholic Women Priests
arcwp.org

Women's Ordination Worldwide
womensordinationcampaign.org

Made in the USA
Columbia, SC
30 April 2022

59614587R00063